The Virginia Law Reporters Before 1880

The Virginia Law Reporters
Before 1880

Edited by
W. Hamilton Bryson

University Press of Virginia
Charlottesville

THE UNIVERSITY PRESS OF VIRGINIA
Copyright © 1977 by the Rector and Visitors
of the University of Virginia

First published 1977

Library of Congress Cataloging in Publication Data
Main entry under title:

The Virginia law reporters before 1880.

    1. Law reporters—Virginia—Biography. 2. Virginia—History. I. Bryson,
William Hamilton, 1941–
KFV2926.C68V57   348′.755′0430922 [B]   77-21451
ISBN 0-8139-0747-0

Printed in the United States of America

Preface

For a long time I wondered who or what was meant by Gratt., Hen. & M., Gilm., and the other references to the older Virginia legal authorities. A cursory investigation revealed that the eighteenth- and nineteenth-century law reporters, whose reports bear their own names, include in their number men of the highest political and legal visibility, such as Thomas Jefferson and George Wythe, as well as persons who are very little known. My curiosity having been aroused, I organized this series of biographical sketches of the Virginia law reporters whose publications are cited by their own names, according to the older custom. This volume brings together through their common interest in law reporting a colonial attorney general, the first law professor in America, a president of the United States, a United States attorney general, a United States Supreme Court justice, many Virginia and federal politicians, Virginia judges, legal scholars, court clerks, a preacher, and a poet. These sketches are arranged according to the order of the official series of *Virginia Reports* with those of the compilers of the miscellaneous reports following in chronological order.

I would like to conclude this preface by acknowledging the generosity of the Faculty Publications Committee of the University of Richmond for their financial support of this book.

W. H. B.

Contents

The Virginia Law Reporters Before 1880

Bushrod Washington

J. Steven McDorman

Bushrod Washington was born in Westmoreland County on June 5, 1762, the son of John Augustine and Hannah Bushrod Washington. John was the younger brother of President George Washington. The president was always especially fond of his nephew Bushrod and made him his sole heir.

Washington studied under tutors at home and in the house of Richard Henry Lee before he entered the College of William and Mary in 1775. In 1778 at the age of sixteen he graduated from William and Mary with an A. B. degree and returned home until 1780. He then went back to Williamsburg to take George Wythe's law course, and he along with John Marshall was initiated into the Society of Phi Beta Kappa in May 1780. But in the fall of that year he left the college to join the Continental army with Colonel John F. Mercer's cavalry troop, and he was present at the Yorktown surrender. After 1781 he studied law for two years in Philadelphia under the distinguished attorney James Wilson, who was to become one of the original members of the United States Supreme Court.

Washington returned to Westmoreland County in 1784 and hung out his shingle, but his law practice was meager. He shortly afterwards moved to Alexandria, where his practice was no more encouraging than it had been in Westmoreland County. It is not clear whether this was because he was a young and inexperienced lawyer or because he spent a vast amount of time on George Washington's private affairs. In 1787 he was elected to the Virginia House of Delegates to represent Westmoreland County and in 1788 became a delegate to the state ratification convention which adopted the United States Constitution in 1789.

He married Julia Ann Blackburn in 1785. She was the

daughter of Colonel Thomas Blackburn, a volunteer aide-de-camp to General Washington. Mrs. Washington was of poor health and very dependent upon her husband, and therefore they took little part in the social functions of Richmond. Nevertheless, she traveled with him everywhere, including his rounds as a circuit judge.

About 1790 Bushrod Washington moved to Richmond, where his practice was more successful. He built a small office near St. Paul's Church west of the Capitol and specialized in equity work. Many young men trained for the law in his office, including Henry Clay. It is during this period in Richmond that Washington wrote up the cases for his two volumes of *Reports of Cases in the Court of Appeals of Virginia*, which covered the years 1790 to 1796. Washington and John Marshall often argued cases against each other while in Richmond, their professional contacts continuing the friendship begun at William and Mary.

In 1798 Robert Brooke, former governor of Virginia, defeated Washington to become the state attorney general. In that same year a vacancy upon the United States Supreme Court occurred when Justice Wilson, Washington's former mentor, died. President Adams felt the appointment should go to a Virginian, and in a letter to Secretary of State Pickering he said either John Marshall or Bushrod Washington would be acceptable but he preferred Marshall because of his conduct in the XYZ Affair and his seniority at the bar. At this time Washington was only thirty-six. President Adams in his reply to Pickering's answer said, "The name, the connections, the character, the merit and abilities of Mr. Washington are greatly respected, but I still think General Marshall ought to be preferred." Marshall declined the appointment to run for Congress and recommended Washington to the position. Washington was then appointed on October 6, 1798. He spent the next thirty-one years as an associate justice of the Supreme Court of the United States.

He was originally appointed to the Southern Circuit, but he took over the Third Circuit in 1803. During his tenure he compiled the opinions of the cases in the Third Circuit which were published in four volumes as *Reports of Cases Determined in the Circuit Court of the United States for the 3rd Circuit from 1803 until 1827.* Horace Binney said of these reports, "I have never thought that his reports of his own decisions did him entire justice, while they in no adequate manner at all fully represent his judicial powers, nor the ready command he held of his learning in the law." Lucius Elmer, an attorney who practiced before Justice Washington, wrote that the justice carried these reports with him in manuscript form before they were printed, remarking "he might some time inadvertently overrule himself, which would be worse than merely overruling some other judge."

He was unacquainted with literature and the arts. Bushrod C. Washington wrote, "Sacrificing general literature, belles lettres, and all that pertained chiefly to adornment for the weightier matters of the law, he became distinguished as a counselor-at-law rather than an advocate," i.e., an orator. Justice Joseph Story wrote, "His mind was solid, rather than brilliant: sagacious and searching rather than quick or eager; slow but not torpid, steady but not unyielding." He went on to say: "If he was not as profound as some, he was more exact than most men . . . . . He indulged not the rash desire to fashion the law to his own views; but to follow out its percepts with a sincere good faith and simplicity." Binney, who practiced in his court for twenty years, said: "His mind was full, his command of all about him indisputable. His learning and acuteness were not only equal to the profoundest argument, but carried the counsel to depths which they had not penetrated." Lucius Elmer also said: "Manners, language, spoken and written were simple and free of arrogance. He regarded only the essential merits of a case, without being influenced by any of its surroundings; knew the cause only by the evidence and decided it by the law." He also commented that Judge Washington was "kind and pleasant in court to the lawyers."

In appearance Bushrod Washington was short, negligently dressed, and had long dark hair combed back from his forehead. He overindulged in the use of snuff. However, in the keeping of his records he was very orderly. Over a period of thirty-five years he used a system of filing all of his letters and accounts alphabetically by month and year.

Most of the justices during the tenure of Chief Justice Marshall on the Supreme Court were overshadowed by him, and Washington seems to have been one of them. Washington and Marshall had known each other for twenty years before their association on the bench, and upon Justice Washington's death Marshall wrote: "I had few friends whom I valued so highly. . . . We have been most intimate friends for more than forty years, and never has our friendship sustained the slightest interruption." He went on to say, "no man knew his worth better or deplores the death more than myself."

Both men were Federalists and on constitutional matters both saw eye to eye. The two justices differed in opinion only three times during the twenty-nine years they were on the Supreme Court together, in *Merrimack* (1814), *Ogden* v. *Saunders* (1827), and *Mason* v. *Haile* (1827). Moreover, *Dartmouth College* v. *Woodward* (1819) was the only time Washington added a concurring opinion to Marshall's opinion. Some felt that Washington lacked any independent thought. Justice William Johnston wrote to Jefferson that the "two are commonly estimated as one judge." However, Justice Story wrote that Washington "claimed the right to think for himself and he admitted the same right in others." Moreover, dissenting opinions were not common at this time.

Albert P. Blaustein and Roy M. Mersky in their sketch of Bushrod Washington note that he himself offered a summary of his constitutional law philosophy in the last years of his life. "His conservative Federalism sought to avoid direct conflicts with the right of states. The court had always assumed good will on the part of the state legislatures, in order to avoid giving offense to individual states. Statutes were overruled only when they directly interfered with the operation of the central government. The states could not tax the salaries of federal officers because, however slight the tax might be initially, it opened the way to removing the financial encouragement of able men to work for the government; the same went for state attempts to tax stocks issued under the authority of the Federal government."

Justice Washington favored the abolition of slavery but only with a plan that would be just to both slaves and owners. In 1816 he became the first president of the American Colonization Society, whose aim was to colonize freed Negroes on the coast of Africa. Washington held this position until his death thirteen years later. In 1821, however, he was the subject of a vicious attack for selling fifty-four slaves from Mount Vernon, separating some of them from their families. When George Washington died, instead of emancipating his slaves, he left them to his nephew with the hope that they would be freed after the death of Martha Washington. However, when she died, Bushrod was not in a financial position to free them and pay them wages or replace them. The slaves who were expecting to be freed were disappointed; this led to resentment, insubordination, and rebelliousness. Washington was thus led to selling some of them, and for this he was criticized by outsiders who were unaware of the problems. Washington defended himself in letters in the Baltimore *Federal Republican* and in *Niles Weekly Register.*

Bushrod Washington was a member of the Episcopal church and a vice-president of the American Bible Society. He received honorary doctorates of laws from Princeton, Pennsylvania, and Harvard. Washington died on November 26, 1829, in Philadelphia, where he was performing his duties as circuit justice. His wife died two days later. They are buried at Mount Vernon.

Sources: L. Friedman and F. L. Israel, *Justices of U.S. Supreme Court* (New York, 1969), 1: 243-66; *DAB*, s.v. "Washington, Bushrod"; J. Story, "Sketch of the Character of Bushrod Washington" in W. W. Story, *Miscellaneous Writings of Joseph Story* (New York, 1972); T. R. B. Wright, *West-*

moreland Co., Va. (Richmond, 1912), "Address of Lawrence Washington," pp. 20-29; J. Hopkinson, *Eulogium . . . of . . . Bushrod Washington* (Philadelphia, 1830); *Am. Journ. Leg. Hist.* 4 (1960): 34-48; *Tyler's Qtly.* 4 (1922): 32-35; *Green Bag* 9 (1897): 329-35; H. Binney, *Bushrod Washington* (Philadelphia, 1858).

William Brockenbrough

David A. Powers III

William Brockenbrough, noted judge, law reporter, and politician, was born on July 10, 1778, at Tappahannock in Essex County. He was one of the six children of Dr. John Brockenbrough and Sarah Roane Brockenbrough. His father was a well-known surgeon in the Virginia navy during the Revolution and also a justice of the Essex County Court; thus he was exposed to the law at an early age.

As a child Brockenbrough was very precocious, and he advanced quickly in his studies. He entered the College of William and Mary at age sixteen, then studied law there, and began the practice of law immediately upon the completion of his studies. In 1802 at the age of twenty-four Brockenbrough made his political debut by being elected to represent Essex County in the House of Delegates.

Brockenbrough was led into politics, no doubt, by his first cousin, Spencer Roane, who with Thomas Ritchie, the editor of the Richmond *Enquirer*, was the leader of the Richmond Junto. Roane was the son-in-law of Patrick Henry; the *Enquirer* was a newspaper of national importance. The Richmond Junto was one of the nation's most powerful and effective leadership groups, and Brockenbrough was a member of it until his death in 1838. It was one of the staunchest supporters of states' rights. It had full control of Virginia politics and carried much influence throughout the nation as a voice for Jeffersonian ideas.

After two years in the House of Delegates, Brockenbrough was appointed to the Council of State in May 1803. He served there for the next six years. The Council advised the governor on all important matters; his appointment makes it clear that by 1803 he was established securely as a member of the Richmond

Junto. From 1807 to 1809 he represented Hanover County in the General Assembly.

During these years he also began his legal writing and published a number of essays on constitutional issues. He used the pseudonym of "Aristogiton" to attack federalism and to show his views supporting states' rights in the Jeffersonian tradition. In these he was greatly influenced by the ancient Greek essays of Harmodious and Aristogiton in opposition to the tyrants of Athens. His essays were favorably received and "greatly admired at the time for the originality and depth of their views." He continued to write in this style throughout his career.

In 1809 the legislature abolished the old district courts and established a system of fourteen superior courts, increasing the number of circuits and creating a need for new judges. These judges were chosen by joint vote of both houses of the legislature with subsequent appointment by the governor. William Brockenbrough was one of them; he was assigned to the thirteenth circuit (Tazewell, Russell, Lee, Washington, Wythe, Grayson, and Montgomery counties). He assumed his new post and did a capable job; three years later, in 1812, he was transferred to the more important and prestigious circuit which included the city of Richmond and the surrounding counties. The circuit judges also sat en banc as the General Court. It was here that he spent most of his judicial life.

In 1815 and 1826 Brockenbrough published two volumes of reports of cases in the General Court, most of them being of criminal appeals. The General Court had a limited civil jurisdiction, but its primary function was to serve as the court of last resort in criminal matters. The first volume was edited jointly with Hugh Holmes, a brother on the bench of this court; it covered the period 1789 to 1814 and was only 336 pages long, with neither a preface nor an index. The second volume, which was done by Brockenbrough alone, was twice as long though it covered a shorter span of time, 1815 to 1826. This was introduced by an essay entitled "Brief Sketch of the Courts of this Commonwealth" and was concluded with indexes to both volumes. These reports are usually cited by their title, *Virginia Cases*, rather than by the reporters' names.

Judge Brockenbrough's position on the bench did not deter his political activities to any great degree. In 1818 he was appointed to the Rockfish Gap Commission to select a site for the proposed University of Virginia. He and his fellow commissioners, among whom were his co-editor Hugh Holmes, former presidents Jefferson and Madison, and the omnipresent Spencer Roane, chose Charlottesville, which, of the suggested locations, happened to be the closest one to Monticello.

In 1816 Judge Brockenbrough was appointed one of the official revisors of the Virginia code. The others were Roane, John Coalter, Robert White, and B. W. Leigh. The new code was seen through the press in 1819 by Leigh. Brockenbrough was a presidential elector in 1817, 1821, 1825, and 1829. He was elevated to the Supreme Court of Appeals in 1834 and sat there until his death in 1838. Many of his decisions are to be found in volumes five through nine of Leigh's *Reports*.

He continued to write political essays, and on March 30 and April 2, 1819, two of his most important essays, published under the name of "Amphityon," appeared in the Richmond *Enquirer*. These essays have recently been reprinted by Gerald Gunther in his book *John Marshall's Defense of McCulloch v. Maryland* (Stanford, 1969). Brockenbrough attacked Marshall for attempting to extend the authority of the federal courts. He was not dealing with minor points relating to the banking issues but was discussing constitutional theories, and Marshall felt obliged to respond to Brockenbrough's Jeffersonian arguments with anonymous essays of his own. It was a scholarly debate over fundamental principles. These essays amply demonstrate the deep intellects of both Marshall and Brockenbrough.

Judge William Brockenbrough was married to Judith White and had three children. His son, John White Brockenbrough, was a distinguished federal judge and afterwards a member of the Confederate Congress; he founded a law school in Lexington which later was merged with Washington and Lee University and published a volume of federal decisions. His older daughter, Mary, married Willoughby Newton, and his other daughter the Reverend John Peyton McGuire. The judge's brother, Dr. John Brockenbrough, was also prominent; a member of the Richmond Junto and president of a bank, he built the house at Twelfth and Clay streets in Richmond which later became the executive mansion of the Confederacy and is now part of the Confederate Museum.

B. B. Minor described the judge as "a tall, dignified and commanding person, but not particularly handsome. He had something of a cross in his eyes, which gave them a peculiar expression." An anonymous enemy called him "a narrow minded, beady eyed old fool," but an admirer thought he was "a strong, vigorous man, strongly marked with common sense and integrity." It was also said that "no one could know him without being struck by the simplicity of his manners, the kindness and warmth of his feelings, and the strength and purity of his principles." On December 11, 1838, Judge William Brockenbrough died in Richmond at the age of sixty-one. He was buried at White Plains, King William County.

Sources: Southern Historical Society Papers 27 (1899): 350–65; *Va. Law Register* 5 (1900): 731–39; *Va. Mag. Hist. Biog.* 78 (1970): 190, 193, 194, 82 (1974): 100–113; *Nat. Cyc. Am. Biog.* 19 (1926): 316; E. G. Swem and J. W. Williams, *Reg. of General Assembly* (Richmond, 1918) pp. 57, 60, 72, 74; *Va. Acts of Assembly 1816–17*, c. 17. s. 4, p. 23; *Journ. Ho. of Del. 1817–18*, pp. 9, 10; G. Gunther, ed., *John Marshall's Defense; Stanford Law Rev.* 21 (1969): 449–55; MS genealogical notes (1968), pp. 368–71, of John Brockenbrough Offley of Williamsburg.

Hugh Holmes

Howard T. Macrae, Jr.

Hugh Holmes was born on November 8, 1768, at Mary Ann Furnace in York County, Pennsylvania. His father, Joseph Holmes, had emigrated to Pennsylvania from northern Ireland, and Hugh was the eldest son of a family that included four sons and five daughters. His mother was Rebecca Hunter Holmes. Joseph Holmes later moved to Winchester, Virginia, where he established himself as a merchant. During the Revolution, he was a colonel of the Second Battalion of the Frederick County militia and was given charge of the prisoners of war held in Winchester.

Hugh's brother David was a member of the House of Representatives during the Fifth through Tenth Congresses, for a period of twelve years. In 1809 President Madison appointed him the first governor of Mississippi, and he was senator from Mississippi at the time of his death in 1832. Another brother, Andrew Hunter Holmes (1789–1814), was a lawyer, having been educated both at Princeton and the College of William and Mary. Little is known about Hugh Holmes's early life and education. However, it appears that he attended the College of William and Mary in about 1789.

On December 20, 1791, Hugh Holmes married Elizabeth Briscoe, the daughter of Colonel Gerard and Margaret Baker Briscoe of Frederick County, Virginia. Another daughter of the Briscoes, Eleanor, married Archibald Stuart (1757–1832), who was destined to serve with Holmes as a judge of the General Court of Virginia. Their son, Alexander Hugh Holmes Stuart, the nephew and namesake of Hugh Holmes, served as a member of the Virginia House of Delegates (1836–39; 1873–79), the United States House of Representatives (1841–43), and the Virginia Senate (1857–61), and was secretary of the interior in the cabinet of Millard Fillmore (1850–53).

Holmes was admitted to the Frederick County bar in 1789 and the Jefferson County (now West Virginia) bar on November 11, 1801. Of his private practice of law and the practice existing in contemporary Virginia, one colorful episode commends itself. The occasion was a case being tried in an Augusta court, in which the opposing counsel was the quick-tempered Gabriel Jones, who was at the time the most prominent lawyer in the western reaches of the Commonwealth. Hugh Blair Grigsby relates the tale. "Holmes was mischievous and witty, and contrived to get Jones into a furious passion, when he became very profane. After hearing Jones for some time, the court consulted together in order to determine what steps should be taken to preserve its dignity. To think of punishing Lawyer Jones was out of the question; so the presiding judge gave it as the decision of the court, 'that if Mr. Holmes did not quit worrying Mr. Jones and making him curse and swear so, he should be sent to jail.' "

Though his profession was that of a lawyer, Hugh Holmes, like many of his fellow Virginia attorneys of the period, participated actively in politics. Insofar as it can be determined, Holmes first held elective office in 1795, when at the age of twenty-seven he was mayor of Winchester and went to Richmond to serve the first of four successive sessions, 1795 to 1799, in the Virginia Senate representing the district including Frederick, Berkeley, Hampshire and Hardy counties. He was absent from the General Assembly for a period of three years, during which time he served as a Republican elector in the Electoral College of 1800, which saw the acrimonious struggle between Jefferson and Burr for the presidency. Holmes returned to the General Assembly in 1802, but this time serving in the House of Delegates for four successive sessions, 1802 to 1806, representing Frederick County. He was elected Speaker of the House of Delegates in 1803 at the age of thirty-five. Holmes held the Speakership until December 1805, when he resigned after having been elected by the General Assembly to be judge of the General Court. In addition to these political offices, Holmes was listed on the rolls of the adjutant general in 1804 as a major in the Third Regiment of Cavalry of the Virginia militia.

In a letter to Archibald Stuart dated April 8, 1801, the newly inaugurated President Jefferson discusses the qualities he was looking for in a man to appoint as a district attorney for the western district of Virginia. As to the candidates for appointment, Jefferson said, "let them be the most respectable and unexceptional possible; and especially let them be republican," as, "the only shield for our Republican citizens against the federalism of the courts." As a fitting candidate, the new president suggested Hugh Holmes, but he feared that the great distance to be traveled to the seat of the court would deter Holmes's acceptance, and the appointment was not made. The personal bond between Holmes and Jefferson can perhaps best be illustrated by the fact that the home Judge Holmes constructed for himself in Winchester was built on a plan furnished by Jefferson.

If politics played a part in the selection of federal judicial officials in the early nineteenth century, the contemporary Virginia judicial system has been described as a "rigid and self-perpetuating oligarchy." Many of the Virginia judges were members or former members of the General Assembly at the time of their election, or were related to those already elected to the bench. Holmes was Speaker of the House of Delegates when he was elected to the General Court bench on December 6, 1805. This was less than two years after his brother-in-law, Archibald Stuart, had been appointed to the same court. Though Holmes resigned as Speaker after his judicial selection in December 1805, he completed his term as delegate, presumably holding office in both the legislative and judicial branches at the same time.

At that time, the General Court was vested with supreme appellate jurisdiction in criminal matters, while the Court of Appeals exercised appellate jurisdiction in civil cases. Virginia maintained a "double-headed court system" for hearing appeals in criminal and civil matters until 1852, when the General Court was abolished. In 1809 the General Assembly created circuit courts or superior courts of law in each county of the Commonwealth. At the time of Holmes's death in 1825, Virginia had been divided into fifteen circuits each containing about seven counties. Each of the fifteen judges of the General Court was assigned to a circuit, and Judge Holmes was assigned to the Superior Court of Law for the Ninth Circuit in Winchester.

The General Court had its origins in the earliest days of seventeenth-century Virginia. However, reporting in the General Court did not begin until 1730. For the most part, the reporters were able lawyers and took an active part in the political life of the state. Such was the case with Judges Brockenbrough and Holmes, whose collaboration produced a volume that reported the cases heard in the General Court for the period between 1789 and 1814. This volume is classified as "1 Virginia Cases" or "3 Virginia Reports" in the current reporter series.

Aside from being brethren of the state's supreme criminal tribunal, the association of Hugh Holmes and William Brockenbrough, also a William and Mary alumnus, can be traced to 1802–3 when they both served in the House of Delegates. Later they both served as members of the Board of Commissioners for the University, which was created by an act of the General Assembly on February 21, 1818, in order to select a site for the University of Virginia and make all the plans, rules, curriculum, and regulations necessary. They thus joined with Jefferson in making preparations for the latter's pet project. As Virginia's preeminent politician lobbying to have the new University located in his native Charlottesville, Jefferson naturally chose as commissioners those most closely allied to him and in tune with his ideas.

The collection of cases compiled by Holmes and Brockenbrough relates mainly to the penal laws of the Commonwealth, since that was the primary function of the General Court, but they are not concerned exclusively with criminal matters. The extremely important constitutional case of *Kamper* v. *Hawkins*, 1 Va. Cas. 11 (1793), which is one of the main pillars supporting the right of judicial review in Virginia, is also contained in their work. The groundwork for judicial review in Virginia had been laid in the earlier cases of *Commonwealth* v. *Caton*, 4 Call (8 Va.) 5 (1782), and *The Cases of the Judges*, 4 Call (8 Va.) 135 in 1788, although decisions favorable to the legislature and judicial temperateness conspired to prevent either from being a landmark case.

Hugh Holmes died in Winchester on January 19, 1825, at the age of fifty-six. He was buried in the old Presbyterian church cemetery and reinterred in Mount Hebron Cemetery in Winchester in 1912.

Sources: Wm. & Mary Qtly., 1st ser. 16 (1907): 120, 27 (1919): 234; *DAB*, s.vv. "Holmes, David" and "Stuart, Alexander Hugh Holmes"; E. G. Dodson, *Speakers and Clerks of Va. House of Delegates* (Richmond, 1956), p. 43; J. E. Norris, *Hist. of Lower Shenandoah Valley* (Berryville, 1972), pp. 193, 336, 351; H. B. Grigsby, *Hist. of Va. Fed. Convention 1788* (New York, 1969), 2:17, 18; *Cal. of Va. State Papers*, 8:275 and 9:75, 190, 410; Swem and Williams, *Reg. of General Assembly*, pp. 45, 47, 49, 52, 60, 62, 64, 67; *Va. Mag. Hist. Biog.* (1900), 8:125; P. L. Ford, *Works of Jefferson* (New York, 1905), 9: 247–48.

Daniel Call

Arthur G. Smith

Although Daniel Call was highly respected both personally and professionally in his lifetime, he is today unknown except as a law reporter. He lived to be seventy-five, but not much remains to tell of his life.

Daniel Call was born in Dinwiddie County in 1765, the son of Daniel Call, Sr. Apparently Call began the practice of law in Petersburg and sometime after 1793 moved to Richmond. His first wife was Elizabeth Taliaferro, who was the sister-in-law of George Wythe. He and Elizabeth had a daughter, Anne, in 1793. Anne married William Cameron in 1813 in Richmond. Call's first wife did not live long, and sometime before 1798 he married Lucy Nelson Ambler, who was the sister-in-law of John Marshall. They had a daugher, Elizabeth Jacquelin Call, who married Daniel N. Norton in 1818.

Daniel Call was a tall, thin man with a very large mouth. Loosely jointed, his arms had a great swing when he walked. In 1798 he bought a small frame house located at the southeast corner of Ninth and Broad streets in Richmond, facing Capitol Square. Call lived there until 1820 when he moved into a house at the corner of Eighth and Marshall streets, where he lived for the rest of his life. The first house was sold by his daughter in 1849 and moved on rollers to its present location at the southeastern corner of Madison and Grace; the second house was torn down in the 1930s. He was the original owner of pew sixty-six in Monumental Church.

Call's legal practice was a general one but included much real property work. He was co-executor of the estate of Jacquelin Ambler, his father-in-law. He represented J. H. Norton, the agent for John Norton and Sons of London, and the estates of Joseph Darmsdatt, Thomas M. Randolph, and Robert Means. Call associated Henry Clay with him in 1822 in order to settle Means's claims to various military lands in Ohio. He also represented Sir Peyton Skipwith of Mecklenburg County and various clients from Baltimore and New York.

Daniel Call (or possibly his father) was elected from Brunswick, Mecklenburg, and Powhatan counties to the United States House of Representatives in 1792, but he seems not to have taken his seat. Much later, in 1827, he was again politically active; in this year he was elected a delegate from Richmond to a political convention to oppose the candidacy of Andrew Jackson for president.

Call's only published writings are his six volumes of reports of cases in the Virginia Court of Appeals. The first three volumes were published in 1801, 1802, and 1805 more or less as the cases were being heard. Volume one was dedicated to George Wythe, chancellor of the Court of Chancery, and volume two to Edmund Pendleton, president of the Court of Appeals. Wythe came first probably because of his family connections with Call but perhaps also because Wythe was the more scholarly of the two. These first three volumes were republished in 1824 by Joseph Tate and in 1854 by Lucian Minor.

Call published the last three volumes in 1833 in order to fill in gaps in the series of Virginia reports before the time of those of Hening and Munford. They contain cases primarily from 1779 to 1806, but there are a few later ones plus four cases from the United States circuit court for Virginia. Volume four, which is dedicated to St. George Tucker, begins with biographical sketches of the early judges of the Court of Appeals. The final volume is dedicated to all of the judges. All six volumes of Call's reports were reedited in 1902 by the Michie Company.

Call had a long and successful life at the Richmond bar and was loved and respected by the brilliant coterie of lawyers who practiced there. He died in Richmond on May 20, 1840, and was buried in Shockoe Cemetery. His grave lies between those of two lifelong friends, John Marshall and George Fisher.

Sources: Wm. & Mary Qtly., 1st ser. 26 (1917): 99; M. W. Scott, *Houses of Old Richmond* (Richmond, 1941) pp. 38–41; *Va. Mag. Hist. Biog.* 5 (1898): 74; *Green Bag* 10 (1898): 16; *Cal. of Va. State Papers*, 5: 450; W. A. Christian, *Richmond* (Spartanburg, 1973), p. 110; Norton/Call, Cameron, and Catterall MSS in the Valentine Museum, Richmond; *South in the Building of the Nation*, 11: 162.

William Waller Hening

Samuel M. Walker, Jr.

William Waller Hening, son of David and Mary Hening, was born in 1767 in Culpeper County. He was one of at least four children in a farming family and was educated by the Reverend John Price and by Adam Goodlett, who taught the young Hening classics in 1784. He probably read law with a practicing attorney before being admitted to the bar in April 1789 in Fredericksburg. His law practice in this area was successful, and in 1791 he moved his residence from Spotsylvania County into Fredericksburg.

Hening moved his law practice to the Charlottesville area in 1793, living first in Albemarle County and then in the town on what is now University Avenue. Here he also dealt in a small amount of real estate and acquired a distillery with which his name was long associated. He made the acquaintance of his neighbor Thomas Jefferson, who no doubt was the man who interested him in editing the statutes of colonial Virginia. This task was begun shortly after Hening left Charlottesville, and its realization perhaps would not have been successful without Jefferson's encouragement and library. Also one might conjecture that Jefferson was instrumental in Hening's election in 1804 to represent Albemarle County in the House of Delegates and in his elevation to the Council of State in 1806.

Hening moved to Richmond in order to perform his duties on the Council of State; his initial residence was in Henrico County and later he moved into the city. While in Richmond, Hening became an active Mason and held the position of Grand Master of Masons in Virginia in 1805–6. Hening resigned his place on the Council of State in 1810 in order to accept the appointment as clerk of the Superior Court of Chancery for the Richmond District. This was done, as he said, to meet "the imperious calls of a large and helpless family." He was married to Agatha Matilda Banks and was the father of seven children. He retained his clerkship until his death in 1828. During the War of 1812 he also held the office of deputy adjutant general of Virginia. However, he was censured by the governor and the House of Delegates in 1814 for exceeding his authority, and he resigned soon thereafter.

In Richmond, Hening apparently did not practice law but attempted to support himself and his family on the inadequate salaries from his public offices and from his legal writing. He was unfortunately a victim of the hazards of the publishing world and was always in financial straits. William J. Van Schreeven has said that "shortly before his death he had mortgaged and lost all of his property including his expensive library, and he even mortgaged his legal fees." Thus the clerkship he undertook did not save him from financial ruin; he likely impoverished himself during the years he spent collecting materials to be used in his *Statutes at Large*, for which he was never reasonably compensated.

It is interesting to note that in 1814 an information was filed and a capias issued against Hening as clerk of the chancery court seeking his removal for breach of good behavior in office. He was accused of misappropriating funds of the court by withdrawing money by checks payable to himself in a total amount of $10,000. As receiver of the court, he was not supposed to draw checks without authority of the court but had done so over a period of a year and a half. The case was sent up to the General Court on a procedural point and reversed; therefore, no clue as to the merits of the case was given, but since he remained in the office for fourteen more years, it is safe to assume that the outcome was favorable to Hening. One possible and logical explanation for the problem is that since he, as clerk, was allowed a commission of 1½% on all moneys brought into court or deposited to his credit in the bank, he merely withdrew his commission as he was entitled to do but did so without the approval of the court, thus violating a procedural rule of his office but not a criminal law.

William Waller Hening was one of the most prolific legal writers of his day. His range covered reports, statutes, and treatises. Hening and William Munford jointly edited four volumes of reports of the Virginia Supreme Court of Appeals, which covered the years 1806 to 1810. Also there are many cases from this same period from the Richmond chancery court. As clerk of this latter court, Hening was in an excellent position to find and report the more interesting decisions of Chancellor Creed Taylor, a learned and respected judge. With the exception of the opinions of George Wythe and Brockenbrough Lamb, these are the only lower court equity reports from Virginia in print.

Another notable feature of Hening and Munford's *Reports* is the attempt to establish a system of advance sheets; this was the first such effort in Virginia. Their system was almost the same as the modern one; the only difference was that when the last advance sheet of the volume was delivered, it was accompanied by a new title page, index, and table of cases so that subscribers could have them bound. In the Virginia State Library there is a copy of the first installment with the original title page dated Richmond, 1807. This experiment was abandoned after the first volume because the Supreme Court of Appeals began sitting in three terms each year and there was not time between the March and April terms to issue any printed reports. The four volumes of Hening and Munford's *Reports* were condensed and annotated in 1857 by Lucian Minor.

Hening's most famous and most important single work is, of course, the *Statutes at Large*. For years he had collected early Virginia "fugitive sessions acts," but it seems that the major impetus to his compiling the *Statutes* came from Thomas Jefferson. Jefferson had wanted to publish the laws of Virginia but was not able to do so. Thus, when Hening wrote Jefferson suggesting that he, Hening, compile the laws, Jefferson freely lent him his collection; many of the manuscripts were so old and fragile they could not be moved from Monticello. Jefferson also expressed complete confidence in Hening's ability to perform the task. Hening combined his collection of laws with that of Jefferson and began the task that led to thirteen printed volumes. He worked long and hard on the job, so much so that his eyesight suffered and his finances as well. The *Statutes* consisted in the final analysis of more than just the laws of Virginia, for they contain proclamations, charters, extracts of records of the General Court, and other valuable historical materials.

The first volume was published in 1809 and the last in 1823, the complete work covering the years 1619 to 1792. It is interesting to note the historian's approach which was taken by this scholar. For example, Hening provides a lesson in the history of the English language, interpretations of historical events, and an insight into the workings of early colonial society in Virginia in his preface to the first volume. Hening believed the best and most accurate way to study the history of a society was through a study of its laws and their development; it seems that this goal, rather than a mere collection of old laws, was his purpose in compiling the *Statutes at Large.*

Hening's other work in the area of legislation was in the capacity of one of the revisors of the Virginia Revised Code of 1819. He and William Munford served as assistants to Benjamin Watkins Leigh on this important project.

Hening's earliest work was a manual or treatise for justices of the peace, *The New Virginia Justice.* The first edition appeared in 1795 and was an instant success. There had been only two earlier handbooks for justices and magistrates, one by Webb published in 1736 and one by Starke in 1775. Both of these were much out of date as a result of independence, a new constitution, and the new Code of 1794. Hening issued enlarged editions in 1799 and in 1810. A substantially revised edition was published in 1820 in order to take into account the changes in the law made by the Revised Code of 1819. The final edition appeared in 1825 with the title *The Virginia Justice.* This work was the standard one, in fact the only one, on the subject, until 1838 when J. A. G. Davis published his treatise on criminal law.

The 1825 edition of Hening's *Justice* involved the author in a bitter fight with the publisher, Peter Cottom, the Council of State, and the governor, who were to distribute copies to all Virginia magistrates pursuant to an act of January 7, 1825, and Thomas Ritchie, the printer and a member of the Richmond Junto. Hening's view of the situation was that in October 1825, when the Council of State refused to accept the 3,000 copies agreed upon, they were justified because the paper chosen by Cottom was inferior and his binding job was poor. So Hening offered to supply a new edition to the state and sold this edition to Cottom for sale to the public. Then a month later as the result of some back-room politics, the books were accepted and Cottom was paid rather than Hening. This made it possible for Cottom to pay Ritchie's company for the printing work it had done. Everyone knew of the connection between the Richmond Junto and the Council of State. Hening felt that he was the loser and published a bitter comment in the form of a pamphlet entitled *A View of the Conduct of the Executive of Virginia.*

Hening supplemented his handbook for Virginia justices by compiling *The American Pleader and Lawyer's Guide.* Volume one was published in 1811 and volume two in 1826. A third was contemplated, but he did not live to do it.

In 1823 Hening published the first American edition of Richard Francis's *Maxims in Equity* and in 1824 the first American edition of Thomas Branche's maxims, *Principia Legis et Aequitatis.* Also in the latter year he edited William Noy's *The Principal Grounds and Maxims of the Laws of England.* Hening's job of editing these works required great diligence because, as he said in his preface to Branche's work, he found numerous errors and false translations from the Latin.

Hening's life at the bar in Fredericksburg and in Charlottesville was peaceful and prosperous. However, the remainder of his life, which he spent in Richmond as the clerk of the chancery court and a legal writer, was characterized by financial disappointments punctuated with public feuds. It is a pity that his last literary effort was the embittered public complaint following his troubles in 1825, and it is sad to remember that he died a pauper. However, his intellectual achievements were recognized in his own day, as they are today, by both lawyers and historians.

Referring to Hening's *Statutes*, George Bancroft wrote, "No other state in the Union possesses so excellent a work on its legislative history." C. M. Andrews said that the *Statutes* are "the greatest and the essential collection of original material for Virginia history." Possibly the finest tribute to Hening came from William J. Van Schreeven, Virginia state archivist, when he said: "We can rightfully attribute to Hening a substantial place in the development of Southern scholarship. He belongs to that small band of obscure scholars whose works are continuously used and quoted, but whose lot it has been to be eclipsed by the interpretations and conclusions based in part upon their labors. It can be said that it is now virtually impossible to write a state or local history of early Virginia, or to treat of its institutional, social, political, and economic development from the earliest beginnings without somewhere making citations to the work of William Waller Hening."

On April 1, 1828, at age sixty-one, Hening died in poverty at the home of one of his sons in Richmond; he was buried in Shockoe Cemetery. His wife followed him only nine days later.

Sources: W. K. Winfree, personal notes and conversations; W. K. Winfree, "Acts Not in Hening's Statutes, with a Biographical Sketch of W. W. Hening" M.A. thesis, Wm. & Mary, 1959; *DAB*, s.v. "Hening, William Waller"; *Wm. & Mary Qtly.*, 2d ser. 22 (1942): 161-64; *Tyler's Qtly.*, 1 (1919): 20; *Va. L. Reg.*, new ser. 13 (1927): 25-37; *Va. Cases*, 1: 324–29; Swem and Williams, *Register of the General Assembly*, pp. 64, 66; J. S. Moore, *History of Richmond Royal Arch Chapter No. 3* (Richmond, 1911), pp. 35, 40, 51, 65, 126; *Cal. of Va. State Papers*, vols. 9, 10, passim.

William Munford

Pamela I. Gordon

William Munford, the only son of Colonel Robert and Anne Beverley Munford, was born August 15, 1775, in Mecklenburg County. Munford's ancestors were prominent in the early history of Virginia, and his father was a distinguished patriot in the Revolutionary War. Colonel Munford was also a playwright and poet who published a collection of plays and poems. From his father, William inherited a love of poetry, and his own literary abilities exceeded those of his father.

When Munford's father died in 1784, the family plantation, Richland, was encumbered with debt. Despite their poor circumstances, Munford's mother was determined that her nine-year-old son would receive a classical and liberal education. She sent Munford to the Petersburg Academy where even at that early age he displayed his love of letters. After three years Munford left the academy and attended the grammar school connected with the College of William and Mary. In 1790 the family's financial circumstances were such that it appeared that Wiliam would have to leave school. Fortunately for the boy, George Wythe, upon hearing of his predicament, took him into his home in Williamsburg. On June 13, 1790, Munford, in anticipation of Wythe's offer, wrote to his friend John Coalter, who was later to become a judge of the Supreme Court of Virginia: "My great resource is Mr. Wythe. If I live with him, I should at the same time think a great point gained, and be highly pleased. Indeed, from some conversations we have had together, I think it likely he will agree. If so, your friend's fortune is made. Nothing could advance me faster in the world than the reputation of having been educated by Mr. Wythe; for such a man as he casts a light all around him."

While living with Wythe, Munford studied Greek, Spanish, and Italian, and from Wythe, Munford acquired his lifelong interest in Homer. Wythe's generosity made it possible for Munford to finish his education at William and Mary, graduating with high honors. He then began the study of law under Wythe.

In 1792 when Wythe was appointed judge of the High Court of Chancery, Munford accompanied him to Richmond to continue his legal studies. However, in 1793 Munford returned to William and Mary to attend law lectures under St. George Tucker because Wythe was too busy as a judge to instruct him. In 1794 the lack of financial resources forced him to return to his native county where he established a successful law practice.

Munford entered politics by seeking membership in the Electoral College of 1796. Some of Munford's political views were revealed in a letter he wrote to General Joseph Jones of Dinwiddie County, in which Munford asked the general for his support. Munford stated that he disapproved of Jay and the Jay Treaty, but he promised that such disapproval would not deter him from supporting Washington for the presidency. However, if Washington refused, Munford said his support would go to Jefferson.

In the following year Munford became a political figure himself when he was elected to represent Mecklenburg County in the House of Delegates. Four years later, in 1802, Munford was elected to the state Senate from his district. In this same year, on February 24, Munford married Sarah Radford of Richmond, daughter of William and Rebecca Radford.

As a legislator Munford was most noted for his support of the extension of the suffrage. In a circular letter to his constituents in 1802, Munford urged the extension of the franchise to all white freemen. This circular began an agitation which was carried on by the opposing side in the *Virginia Gazette*, a Federalist paper. Editions of the *Gazette* on February 23 and 26 and March 2, 1803, quite vigorously opposed

Munford's view on suffrage and his opposition to the establishment of a bank.

Munford's term as a senator ended in 1806 when he was chosen by the legislature to become a member of the Council of State. He then moved his family to Richmond, where he resided until his death in 1825. The year 1806 brought personal sadness to Munford with the death of his friend George Wythe. Munford delivered the address at the funeral in Richmond. In this same year Munford became a reporter of the decisions of the Virginia Court of Appeals. He was an active member of the Richmond Junto. In 1811 Munford's membership in the Privy Council terminated and he became the clerk of the House of Delegates, an office he held for the remainder of his life.

During the intervening years Munford was active in his church and sought to improve the educational system of Virginia. He served as secretary-treasurer of the Convention of the Episcopal Diocese of Virginia from 1815 to 1824. Munford believed that the educational system of Virginia could be improved by changing from a private to a public school system. In 1815 Munford along with Thomas Ritchie, editor of the Richmond *Enquirer*, and Andrew Stevenson, a congressman, called a meeting in Richmond to consider the establishment of a Lancastrian school based on the British public school system. Such a school was established in 1816 from municipal and private funds. The school remained in operation until 1851.

As the years went by Munford's family continued to grow. Munford and his wife, Sarah, were the parents of eight children: George Wythe Munford, father of Brigadier General Thomas Taylor Munford; Anna Rebecca Munford, who married John Sherrard; John Durburrow Munford, father of Beverley B. Munford who acquired national reputation as author of *The Attitude of Virginia Towards Slavery and Secession*; Robert Munford, M.D.; Elizabeth Madison Munford, who married William Preston Peyton; William Preston Munford; Elvira H. Munford, who married first Powhatan

L. Ellis and second Benjamin Howard Peyton; and Carlton Radford Munford. It has been argued that Munford's large family forced him to give up a literary career and establish a law practice instead, but this seems unlikely considering his success in law and politics.

William Munford became a reporter of the decisions of the Supreme Court of Appeals of Virginia in 1806. From that year until 1809 Munford in conjunction with William Waller Hening published four volumes of decisions. Included in the volumes were some cases decided in the Superior Court of Chancery for the Richmond District. In the preface to Hening and Munford's *Reports*, the reporters stated their intention to present the "state of the case and the opinions of the Judges." In reporting the opinions, the authors looked to the notes of the judges which the judges provided for them. These notes were published almost verbatim. To give an accurate statement of the case, the authors referred to the records themselves and the briefs of counsel. Because of the length of some of the arguments of counsel, the reporters condensed the arguments and reported only the substance applicable to the points of law decided. For a few leading cases the reporters gave the arguments of counsel nearly as they were delivered.

From 1810 to 1820 Munford reported six volumes of decisions of the Court of Appeals, working alone. Although he wrote no prefaces to his own volumes, he apparently continued to follow the method of reporting used previously when he was collaborating with Hening.

Munford's fifth volume was published in April 1817. Before his sixth and last volume was published, the judges of the Court of Appeals sent a letter dated December 6, 1819, to the House of Delegates. This letter urged the legislature to appoint someone as reporter who would serve under the authority of the legislature. According to the letter, a competent person would be attracted to the position if an adequate salary was offered. The letter went on to state: "The reports of the decisions of the court of which we are members for nearly three years back, are in arrear and unpublished. The very respectable gentleman who has heretofore published such reports has been prevented by various causes from performing that duty. The accounts of the decisions of that period are, in most instances, locked up in his office . . . . We are of opinion that a suitable character ought to be appointed, under the authority of the legislature, to publish these reports, and that they should be promulgated shortly after the decisions have been made." In 1820 the legislature authorized the Court of Appeals to appoint a proper person to report cases that in the opinion of the court were woth reporting. Francis W. Gilmer became the first reporter appointed by the court, thereby ending Munford's career as a reporter. Munford's reports, therefore, were the last published by private account. Whether Munford's other interests were responsible for his dilatoriness is not known, but he was engaged in other pursuits.

Munford at a very early age acquired a love for the classics, especially Homer. He had been encouraged to study the classics by his father, his mother, and most importantly by his friend, George Wythe. While a student at William and Mary, Munford studied under Charles Bellini, a professor of languages who obtained his position through the help of Thomas Jefferson. Bellini, in writing to Jefferson on April 1, 1799, described the quality of his students with specific reference to Munford: "But above all there is one here at present who is certainly an ornament to human nature. He landed here a few months ago from on board a ship. His name is Monfund [*sic*]. Divest him but of one failing, self-sufficiency, and he would certainly be one of the most perfect creatures that ever came from the hands of the Creator."

In 1798 a volume of Munford's literary works was published in Richmond. This volume, entitled *Poems and Compositions in Prose on Several Occasions*, was the only literary work of Munford's to appear during his lifetime with his name on the title page. It contains twenty poems, some political addresses, a Fourth of July oration delivered in Williamsburg in 1793, and a play.

Munford's most successful literary effort by far was his translation of Homer's *Iliad*. The translation over which Munford labored many years was completed in 1825, several months before he died. However, it was not until 1846 that it gained sufficient recognition to be published. Following its publication a number of reviews, both favorable and unfavorable, appeared in various periodicals. The most important of these reviews was that of C. C. Felton, an eminent Greek scholar of Harvard. Felton prefaced his elaborate review with these words: "A translation of the *Iliad* coming from Virginia does more honor to that ancient Commonwealth than her political dissertations, endless as they are. We have so long been accustomed to political talk from old Virginia, that a purely literary work, having no possible connection with 'the party', strikes us as something unexpected, strange, and surprising." The Greek scholar spoke of Munford's poetic style as "rich, and rhythmical, stately, and often remarkably expressive."

The *Southern Literary Messenger*, a Richmond publication, also carried a review of Munford's *Iliad* in 1846. The author lamented that "a name which had seemed destined to stand high among the literary men of Virginia is now known to the reading public only as it stands in the title page of ten volumes of reports of the Judgments of the Court of Appeals." He also argued that Munford had orginally entered the study of law to acquaint himself with the institutions and laws of his country as any gentleman ought to possess. "If he [Munford] thought of practicing it was probably more as an intellectual exercise, and a trial of forensic ability than as a source of profit." It was, therefore, suggested that Munford's decision to practice law was due to his expensive and growing family. The reviewer concluded that when Munford became a reporter for the Supreme Court of Appeals, "the scholar and poet subsided into a professional drudge." Almost a century later, Richard

Beale Davis argued to the contrary: "It is hard to believe, however, that Munford saw this implied tragedy or even considered drudgery in the situation, for he gave every indication that he loved the law. During his whole life the two interests existed side by side with little evidence of conflict."

Whether or not Munford would have pursued a purely literary career if financial circumstances had permitted is open to conjecture. There is no doubt that Munford loved the classics, and he is reported to have worked on his translation of the *Iliad* while sitting in court as a reporter. Because of his translation, some writers conclude that Munford's greatest achievements were in the field of letters rather than law or public service.

In addition to Munford's reports and his literary works, he compiled *A General Index to the Virginia Law Authorities* and a revision of the Code of Virginia. The *Revised Code of Laws of Virginia*, made in conjunction with William W. Hening and B. W. Leigh, was published in 1819. The *Index* contains points of law extracted from the *Reports* of Washington and Call, the Hening and Munford *Reports*, and the Munford *Reports*. The purpose of the *Index* was two-fold. First, it was to aid the lawyer or judge to find a point of law quickly without having to peruse all of the volumes of the *Virginia Reports*, and second, Munford wanted to provide a convenient way for the layman to acquire some knowledge of law. Like the code revision, the *Index* was published in 1819. In a letter of August 10, 1824, to William H. Fitzwhylsonn, Munford stated that he had almost finished a second volume to his *Index* and hoped to find a publisher in the next month or two. However, this work was never printed.

William Munford was a gentle and modest man of many talents and abilities who to a great extent owed the development of his potential to his friend George Wythe. Munford, who is worthy of recognition as a lawyer, court reporter, legislator, and poet, died on June 21, 1825, in Richmond.

Sources: DAB s.v. "Munford, William"; F. V. N. Painter, *Poets of Va.* (Richmond, 1907), pp. 41-45; J. B. Hubbell, *South in Am. Lit.* (Durham, 1954), pp. 283-287; R. B. Munford, *Richmond Homes* (Richmond, 1936), pp. 1-5; R. M. Baine, *Robt. Munford* (Athens, Ga., 1967); J. McGill, *Beverley Family* (Columbia, S.C., 1956), p. 616; R. B. Davis, "Homer in Homespun," *Southern Literary Messenger*, rev. ser. 1 (1939): 647-51; *Tyler's Qtly.* 3 (1922): 178, 179, 25 (1944): 167-69; *Va. Mag. Hist. Biog.* 78 (1970): 191; *Wm. & Mary Qtly.*, 1st ser. 8 (1900): 153-57, 2d ser. 5 (1925): 11, 8 (1928): 17-31; *No. Am. Rev.* 63 (1846): 149-65; Munford Letterbook, Va. Hist. Soc. MSS 5:2M9235:1; Swem and Williams, *Register of the Genl. Assembly*, pp. 49, 56, 58, 61, 63, 66, 68.

Francis Walker Gilmer

Michael A. Lofaro

Francis Walker Gilmer (1790-1826), the tenth child of a Virginia plantation household, was born on October 9, 1790, at Pen Park, an estate approximately two miles northeast of Charlottesville and near Monticello. Christened Francis Thornton Gilmer, he assumed the name of his uncle Francis Walker after the latter's death in 1806. His father, Dr. George Gilmer, the most prominent physician in Albemarle County, was the associate and friend of Thomas Jefferson and James Madison and served in 1774 as a representative in the House of Burgesses. Francis Gilmer inherited the fine mental qualities of his father but also the weak physical constitution that plagued the entire family. Only two of the ten children lived to be more than fifty years of age, and Francis was not to be numbered in that fortunate minority.

In 1795, after Dr. Gilmer's death at the age of fifty-two, the entire family was scattered throughout Virginia, never to be re-united as a complete family group. Francis, however, remained in Albemarle County until he was eighteen as a guest-ward of some of the neighboring families. During this period the young Gilmer undoubtedly came into contact with many of his father's influential and rather illustrious acquaintances. In the immediate area, in addition to the households of Jefferson and Madison, were the homes of such notables as James Monroe and Colonel Thomas Mann Randolph, Jefferson's son-in-law and governor of Virginia. Also nearby were the residences of Andrew Stevenson, the Speaker of the United States House of Representatives and minister to England, and Dabney Carr, the younger son of a burgess and Revolutionary patriot who married Jefferson's sister. It was Carr, a judge of the Court of Appeals of Virginia, who became perhaps Gilmer's closest friend, next to his lifelong confidant and legal mentor, his brother-in-law William Wirt.

Among these early influences another remarkably talented man should be acknowledged. In 1807 Francis Gilmer became the pupil of James Ogilvie, a wandering Scottish scholar who had emigrated to Virginia early in life and now hoped to found a fine classical school. A brilliant teacher far ahead of his day in terms of using a lecture format as the main pedagogical method for his older students, Ogilvie was an unusually egocentric individual with a great flair for oratory, an ability which seems to have been in no way diminished by his addiction to drugs and alcohol. He later, in fact, journeyed up and down the Atlantic seaboard from 1809 to 1812, giving orations which met with phenomenal success. The brief teacher-pupil relationship grew into a friendship which continued mainly by correspondence until Ogilvie's death by his own hand in 1820. The orator's predominant effect upon Gilmer was the shaping of the latter's public speaking away from the bombast of current rhetoric, with which Ogilvie himself often ornamented his harangues, toward a much more lucid style that was later to serve him well in his arguments before the bar.

By 1809 Gilmer had entered the College of William and Mary to prepare for a career in law. Although also a fairly accomplished amateur botanist by his graduation in June 1810, he regarded this pursuit, as well as the other fields in arts and sciences in which he was to demonstrate no mean expertise, as only engaging avocations, hobbies which entertained while sharpening the wits. By January 1811 he was reading law in Richmond under the tutelage of William Wirt. Wirt had been thrust into national prominence through his appointment by President Jefferson as counsel in the Aaron Burr case in 1807. Throughout his early life, Gilmer seemed to turn instinctively to Wirt for legal criticism and praise, as well as personal guidance and solace.

Gilmer's respect for Wirt stemmed in some measure from

the lawyer's great fortitude in reversing the dissipations of his almost notoriously rakish past. He also considered his older friend a very fit model for emulation in terms of his combination of law and literature. In addition to carrying on an immense legal practice, Wirt was simultaneously trying his hand at the essay, lyric poetry, and drama. Today his best-known literary effort is his *Sketches of the Life and Character of Patrick Henry*. Wirt's oversentimentalized depiction of the fiery lawyer's life still serves as the basis for many current biographical portrayals. His brilliant recreations from scanty notes of the famous speeches of the great orator have made Wirt's versions American classics. That Gilmer was fascinated by Wirt's dual success is hinted at in a letter of June 28, 1813. In it he stated, "I am already panting for the bar," and also, "I have some other schemes of literary occupation in view."

A little more than a year later, Gilmer was to realize the first goal. After being convinced by friends and family that his considerable talents made it unnecessary to move to the Kentucky frontier where there would be little legal competition to eclipse his rising career, Gilmer decided to open his office in Winchester. Before he could enter the public arena, however, the British advanced up the Potomac and burned Washington, D.C. Although he had once fled military service, Gilmer felt this stain upon the nation's honor keenly. He rushed to Richmond to enlist in a battalion under Wirt's command to help defend the city. But the combination of daily drills and the fact that the British subsequently chose to attack Baltimore made military life unattractive to many of the young high-spirited Virginians. Wirt captured their mood quite well in a letter to his wife in which he stated regretfully that "Frank Gilmer, Jefferson Randolph [Jefferson's grandson], the Carrs [probably Peter and Frank, Jefferson's nephews], [Abel P.] Upshur [later United States Cabinet member], and others, have got tired of waiting for the British and gone home."

Home for Gilmer did not mean a permanent return to

Winchester. He continued to put off a full commitment to
the law and instead took advantage of an unparalleled educational opportunity. During the previous summer of 1813
he had met through Jefferson the Abbé Joseph Francisco
Correa de Serra, a Portuguese botanist, scientist, and phi-
losopher of international fame. Now their mutual interest
in botany drew the youth of twenty-four and the man forty
years his senior together. They became traveling compan-
ions in a journey along the Atlantic seaboard from Richmond to Washington and finally to Philadelphia. The Abbé
Correa's companionship and letters of introduction from
Jefferson gave Gilmer access to all the sophisticated scientific and literary salons in these cities. He seems to have enjoyed especially the celebrated "Wistar parties" in Philadelphia which took their name from Dr. Casper Wistar, the
nationally renowned anatomist and then president of the
American Philosophical Society. Gilmer, although a provincial in experience, acquitted himself admirably well.
The letters of the gentlemen and ladies of the Wistar circle
indicate admiration and respect for the accomplished Virginian. It was during this stay in Philadelphia that Gilmer
and the Abbé Correa planned a now mysterious scheme of
travel in Europe which would result in huge financial gain.
The scheme was never enacted. Napoleon's escape from
Elba set Europe into a state of turmoil in which the aging
Correa did not wish to engage and the project was abandoned.

Gilmer spent part of the summer of 1815 in Charlottesville and by August 1 was back in Winchester readying himself for the next court session. Within a few weeks, however,
temptation again appeared in the person of Correa. The
lure of a botanical expedition with the great scientist to com-
mence with excursions in and around Jefferson's summer
house at Poplar Forest, near Lynchburg, in the company
of the former president, could not be ignored. Correa and
Gilmer then proceeded at a leisurely pace through the Car-
olinas and into Georgia. Here the two visited the tribes of

the Cherokee nation, an experience which Gilmer subsequently recorded in his "Reflections on the Institutions of the Cherokee Indians" (1818). In it he touched upon the influence of geography and climate, which he felt contributed to making the Indians different from the whites in both appearance and custom, and as well described their economy and social stratification. Not unexpectedly he was quite interested in the Cherokee legal system and found that its first principle in nearly all matters was that of retaliation. Although somewhat a romantic in taste, Gilmer seemed to have been shocked at times by how few of the traits of Rosseau's "natural man" could be found among the Cherokees. Rather than "noble savages" who lived a life of liberty and equality in the forest primeval, Gilmer found a race he disapprovingly described as a "mixture of insensibility, vulgarity, and vice." In this judgment Gilmer was at one with the majority of contemporary Americans.

Francis Gilmer returned to Virgina by December 3, 1815, but was soon confined to home by illness for most of January. During this period he occupied his time by composing a remarkable little geological treatise entitled "On the Geological Formation of the Natural Bridge in Virginia," which was read before the American Philosophical Society on February 16, 1816. He was the first to suggest the still accepted theory that the bridge was formed by erosion caused by an underground stream. Gilmer's interest in Virginiana eventually led the lawyer to another notable effort—the publication of the first scholarly American edition of Captain John Smith's *General Historie of Virginia* and Smith's *Memoirs* (1819).

Although Gilmer had come back to Winchester determined to launch his legal career, fame came initially, and rather ironically, from the idle hours he devoted to the field of literature. His *Sketches of American Orators* appeared anonymously in the spring of 1816, but he was immediately recognized as its author. In order he treated John Randolph of Roanoke, John Marshall, Thomas Addis Emmett, William Pinkney, Patrick Henry, Littleton Waller Tazewell, and William Wirt. A sketch of Henry Clay was added to the second edition. The volume is important historically as one of the first evaluations of the finest practitioners of America's then most widespread literary endeavor. It is also important to Gilmer's own career. In his criticism and praise of these lawyers, many of whom were the titans of their times, the reader senses much of the calculated genesis of Gilmer's courtroom technique. Eloquence was to be maintained, and more originality and genuine sophistication encouraged, but never at the price of logic. The far too common oratorical workhorses of tirade and rhetoric were to be retired from a strained harness and placed in proper perspective. Gilmer went on to challenge all lawyers to strive to achieve excellence in terms of this model. It certainly would be fair to conclude that he attempted to excel within these same standards.

The study of the pros and cons of the argumentation of these legal greats rapidly produced tangible results. Gilmer, sharing a bit of Wirt's flair for the dramatic, had on the latter's advice postponed his first court appearance in Winchester until he was scheduled to appear in an important case. Wirt termed the debut as nothing less than brilliant and indeed it must have been—a ten-minute summation in his defense of a notorious criminal brought about the acquittal of a man who before the trial had practically been condemned as a horsethief.

Gilmer applied himself diligently to his practice and remained in Winchester for two years. After he discovered at the end of his first year that he could turn a profit fairly easily, he was eager to try his abilities in a more demanding locale such as Baltimore. Upon inspection he found that the opportunities in this city were great—a large population and a dearth of legal talent because William Pinkney was abroad—but also encountered a three-year residency requirement. He rapidly decided upon familiar Richmond as an alternative and had completed the move by the beginning of 1818. Prospects soon proved better even than he dared hope. William Wirt had just become attorney-general of the United States and Gilmer stepped into a considerable part of the substantial practice of his patron. Again he chose an important case for his first foray in the Richmond criminal courts. The young provincial lawyer was appointed defense counsel for the "ex-convict and maniac" Gibson who had committed a bloody murder. The unsympathetic jury seemed to have been an accurate mirror of the outrage and indignation of the public which were focused on the criminal. In his final argument in the long trial Gilmer stated that he had a momentary loss of confidence and his "delivery was embarrassed." Even though in a letter of April 25, 1818, to Dabney Carr he mentions that "I recovered a pace—touched the topics which weaken all circumstantial evidence, & arrayed the cases pretty well," he still pronounced a harsh judgment upon his performance:

some three or four jurors—the Sheriff & Gen. Cocke who was at my side shed tears of pity for me I thought then—but they said they could not help it—I did not satisfy myself at all—& made a poorer speech than any I ever studied at Winchester—the tears notwithstanding. Some praised—& others said nothing—but I was disappointed—The young lawyers to a man in the progress of the cause embodied against me with the attorney general. The jury went out about five o'clock, so we waited till near sunset—no chance of agreeing was the report—Thought I, this was well, as they agreed in five minutes before. The next morning came—still no chance of agreeing—The attorney moved for new evidence to be heard—it was allowed—I excepted to the opinion of the court. The jury then found "guilty of murder in the first degree." But while the verdict was sounding I saw a certain record containing depositions among the papers. I said nothing, but considered the matter—(and by a pair of nice points won a new trial)—Thus I have won the best two in three, with every prejudice, & every opposition in my way and from henceforth I wash my hands of the aforesaid Gibson—whether I have done well or ill—let time determine—I have indulged my vanity.

As the tone of the letter indicates, Gilmer did manage to

soothe his somewhat ruffled self-image by winning a new trial. The notoriety of the case brought Gilmer into prominence as an attorney and assured his fortune. How far his reputation had grown was indicated in another letter on July 9 of that year, a letter which also revealed Gilmer's view of professional ethics:"—A murder had been committed in Nottoway by one of a most powerful family on another highly respectable person with a wife and children. I have been offered 1000$ to prosecute the murderer. . . . I have agreed to prosecute, but without receiving a fee. So that should the prisoner prove his innocence (or justification, for there is no dispute about the fact, the homicide being committed on the court green) I shall be at liberty to withdraw from the cause. For I never will prosecute a man whom—I believe to be innocent." Late in November he was considering running for the legislature, but ultimately he decided against this pursuit for "it might hurt my reputation." All such considerations, however, were forced into the background by the great depression of 1819. His own bank stock for the time was worthless, his older brother Peachy had invested heavily in land just before the bottom dropped out of the real estate market, and the family of another brother, George, was in even more desperate financial trouble. Francis gave as much aid as he could in his newly limited circumstances. He also considered moving the Gilmer clan "to the sunny green of Florida" for he recognized the untapped potential of that territory. Instead, he journeyed to Georgia in the spring to try to recover a large body of land for a client with the expectation of staying on and realizing $40,000 to $50,000 for six months' work. He returned in six weeks after completing the original mission, however, for he saw that the sum to be gained by remaining would not approach the figure he had imagined. A slow rebuilding of the family's and his personal fortune through activity in the courts occupied the majority of Gilmer's time through the end of 1821.

Perhaps his renewed dedication to the law had another

source as well. In many of his letters of 1819 and 1820 he recounted an old bitterness over his rejection by Ellen Randolph, daughter of Thomas Mann Randolph and the favorite granddaughter of Jefferson. She had, it seems, encouraged his love at first, but now treated him with disdain. Although it would be unfair to judge the lady since only Gilmer's comments are available, it is clear that he felt the sting of this unrequited love deeply. His devotion to the law may have provided some comfort for his sensitive nature. He was able, however, to find the time in the summer of 1820, when legal activity was at a low ebb, to produce a noteworthy treatise in another of his avocations—economics. *A Vindication of the Laws Limiting the Rate of Interest on Loans*, Gilmer's sole venture into economic philosophy and practice, was an immediate success. This cogently argued rebuttal of Jeremy Bentham's classic *Defence of Usury* again and again breaks down Bentham's analyses. Gilmer consistently championed the Jeffersonian belief in the natural rights of man and closed the long essay with an appeal to Americans to reject such "foreign" economic beliefs and construct their own system based upon classical models.

The desire to produce *A Vindication* stemmed not from an attempt to win the praise which it did receive from the American economic community, but rather from Gilmer's interest in an openly disputed point in the laws concerning usury. From April 20, 1820, to June 28, 1821, he served as the court reporter for the Virginia Court of Appeals. In his introduction to the cases reported, he commented specifically on only *Taylor v. Bruce*, a case which "was of such novelty and interest, and the law not being settled by the decision, that the Reporter was at the trouble to obtain the notes of one of the Judges, that the arguments as far as practical might be exhibited." At issue was the concept and definition of usury, and Gilmer himself served as counsel for Taylor, the adminstrator of the Holloway estate. *A Vindication* was materially the fruit of the arguments first introduced on behalf of his client and marked Gilmer's continued fight against what he believed to be faulty interpretations of the laws of just lending.

His actual involvement was in the reconsideration of the case, which had already been decided two to one in favor of Bruce, the moneylender. The dissenting opinion when combined with several precedents cited by Call, the original attorney for Taylor, won the retrial in which Gilmer participated with Call as co-counsel. The matter was in contention because Bruce had gained ownership of certain discounted notes from an intermediary named Mertens and not from Holloway himself. Bruce stated that he did not recall that Mertens ever mentioned that he was Holloway's agent and denied knowledge of Holloway's failing business situation. Bruce further stated that the transaction was a purchase from Mertens and not a loan to Holloway. Gilmer argued that the 18 to 25 percent discount on the yearly notes indicated a knowledge of the difficulties of Holloway's firm and the intent to take advantage of these circumstances. Gilmer's reasoning in the case not only paralleled that in his usury essay but revealed why Jefferson noted that the young lawyer was an unusually successful performer before the state Court of Appeals. The following extracts from Gilmer's opening remarks, as he reported them, will transmit the true force of his argumentative style:

Usury is to be inferred from circumstances, or it could never be proved. Courts must be more astute in detecting usurers as they become more cunning in evading the statute. Where a particular badge of usury is sought to be avoided by a new artifice, that artifice must stand in place of the badge. Thus when men endeavour to avoid the suspicion resulting from a communication for a loan, by the interposition of an agent, the communication with the agent shall stand for a communication with the principal. So when they endeavour to escape the inference resulting from employing a special known agent, by contracting thro' a notorious general agent or broker, who publicly negotiates such usurious contracts, that too, must stand in the place of a direct communication for a loan with the party . . . .

It is said not to be enough to shew that Bruce suspected this was a cover to a usurious transaction; that we must prove he actually knew it. We never can prove what B. knew, nor even what he actually suspected . . . .

But whatever may have been Bruce's knowledge or suspicion, it is certain, that in point of fact, these notes were made for the purpose of raising money, and were actually appropriated to that purpose, without any value having been paid for them, before they came to the hands of Bruce, who gave 18 and 25 percent less than their value for them; and this I say is usury per se.

Gilmer supported his comments in detail with a battery of English and American precedents, but the court, still composed of the three original judges, divided along the same lines. Yet there are hints that Gilmer's arguments had a certain effect. Judge Coalter, who with Judge Brooke formed the majority opinion, stated that despite this particular decision, "the law in this important point is not settled." In his affirmed dissent, Judge Roane left no doubt as to his belief as to the correct judgment in the matter: "it is proved to my conception, as clearly as human testimony can do it, that the transaction in question, both in its origin and consummation was founded in usury."

Although the reasons for Gilmer's relatively short term as court reporter are not entirely known, the change in tone from the reporting of other lawyers' cases to the reporting of those in which he actively participated indicates that he yearned for direct legal action. The experience had certainly been worthwhile, but the role was one he felt unsuitable for a prolonged period. Gilmer submitted a set of recommendations regarding the selection of a new reporter only eight months after he assumed the office.

Toward the end of his fourteen-month term as court reporter, Gilmer's thoughts again turned to Florida because of its recent aquisition from Spain. He had his eye on the position of secretary of state for Florida and wrote to Wirt to intercede for him with President Monroe. Much to Gilmer's chagrin, Wirt replied that Monroe had stated in effect that the young barrister was overqualified for the position, that " 'there is no field there worthy of him.' " Gilmer did not linger over this disappointment and kept on with his ever-expanding practice. By December 1823 his success in both the federal and chancery courts resulted in complete financial recovery from the crash of 1819. He was soon able to write to a friend that the fee he collected for one recent case was in excess of $800 cash and to note rather proudly how far he had come since Winchester, where such a sum "is a year's earnings to an obscure provincial."

Gilmer's greatest contribution to his native Virginia was still before him. In November 1823, Jefferson, in conference with Joseph C. Cabell, his lieutenant in the legislature, and with James Monroe, sent a letter to Gilmer asking him to act as commissioner to England for the purpose of securing professors for Jefferson's long-planned University of Virginia. Cabell had been the first choice, but a constitution as weak as Gilmer's own, when added to his political commitments, led him to decline the office. Gilmer felt it his public duty to accede to the request of his friend from Monticello, but was unsure whether to accept the position of professor of law which Jefferson also offered to him. The professorship was by no means to be the reward for undertaking the task, but rather was proferred in complete accord with the qualifications Jefferson stressed that each instructor must have. Each man must not only be an expert in his own field but also be able to work intelligently with other members of the faculty in their particular disciplines. Each must likewise be grounded in history, general linguistics, and philosophy. Gilmer was perhaps the best qualified man in America to fill the chair of law as Jefferson envisioned it. His writings accurately mirrored the wide range of his erudition, and he had become known in Richmond as a lawyer's lawyer because of his nearly total recall of the fine points of the law. Jefferson's faith in his young Albemarle neighbor was complete. Gilmer was empowered to select and hire six professors and was fully responsible for negotiating the salary of each, as well as for the purchase of text-books and scientific apparatus. His mission to Europe lasted from May to November 1824. The selections were the proof of Jefferson's good judgment. Gilmer engaged George Blaettermann (modern languages), Thomas Hewett Key (mathematics), George Long (ancient languages), and Dr. Robley Dunglison (medicane).

The extremely rough sea voyage back to New York induced a severe illness from which Gilmer never fully recovered. Still he strove to fulfill his commission. While in that city he hired Dr. John Patton Emmet to head the programs in natural history (science). Gilmer had thus completed his task and successfully staffed the University of Virginia except for the professorship of law which he had now declined three times. But in late May, approximately eleven weeks after the University had opened on March 7, 1825, Gilmer finally accepted the position, for he felt his own ill health was such that he would be unable to carry on actively in his practice. Unfortunately his condition was even worse than he feared, and he never taught in the institution he helped to establish. On January 1, 1826, he was told that he had an incurable case of pulmonary consumption. He died a bachelor several weeks later on February 25, 1826, at the age of thirty-six, a little more than four months before his friend Jefferson.

It was Jefferson, a critical judge, who best described the potential and growth of Francis Walker Gilmer. In 1815 he said that the young lawyer "will be in future whatever he pleases in either the State, or General Government," and in 1824 that Gilmer was "the best-educated subject we have raised since the Revolution, highly qualified in all the important branches of science, professing particularly that of law." The extraordinary achievements predicted for Gilmer were never fully realized. Yet, despite his physical incapacities, he became, in his short life, an accomplished lawyer, as well as an author, geologist, economist, botanist, and social scientist. The greatest tribute which could be paid to this gentleman of Virginia is that, had he lived, he may have come closest to duplicating the Renaissance-like genius of Thomas Jefferson.

The Writings of Francis Walker Gilmer

[Anon.] *Sketches of American Orators.* Baltimore: Fielding Lucas, 1816.

"On the Geological Formation of the Natural Bridge of Virginia." In *Transactions of the American Philosophical Society*, n.s. 1 (Feb. 1816): 187-92.

"Reflections on the Institutions of the Cherokee Indians, from Observations Made During a Recent Visit to That Tribe: In a Letter from a Gentleman of Virginia to Robert Walsh, Jan.-June 1st. 1817." In the *Analectic Magazine* (July 1818): 36-56.

Edition of *The General Historie of Virginia, New England, and the Summer Iles . . .* , and *The True Travels, Adventures and Observations of Captaine Iohn Smith . . . .* 2 vols. Richmond: Franklin Press, 1819.

[Anon.] *A Vindication of the Laws, Limiting the Rate of Interest on Loans; from the Objections of Jeremy Bentham, and the Edinburgh Reviewers.* Richmond: Franklin Press, 1820.

Reports of Cases Decided in the Court of Appeals of Virginia (from April 10, 1820, to June 28, 1821). Richmond: Franklin Press, 1821.

Sketches, Essays, and Translations. Baltimore: Fielding Lucas, 1828. Posthumous collection, some additions.

Sources: R. B. Davis, *Francis Walker Gilmer* (Richmond, 1939); R. B. Davis, *Intellectual Life in Jefferson's Va.* (Chapel Hill, N.C., 1964); R. B. Davis, *Corresp. of Jefferson and Gilmer* (Columbia, S.C., 1946); *DAB*, s.v. "Gilmer, Francis Walker"; P. A. Bruce, *Hist. of the Univ. of Va.* (New York, 1920); W. P. Trent, *English Culture in Va.* (Baltimore, 1889); E. Woods, *Albemarle Co.* (Charlottesville, 1901); *Southwestern Univ. Bull.*, History number, vol. 21, n.s., no. 3 (1934); *Huntington Library Qtly.*, 12 (1949): 191-205; *Ga. Hist. Qtly.* 27 (1934): 271-84; *Va. Mag. Hist. Biog.*, 46 (1938): 97-111; *Wm. & Mary Qtly.*, 2d ser. 19 (1939): 55-68.

Peyton Randolph

R. Gaines Tavenner

Peyton Randolph, the law reporter who died in 1828, was a member of one of the most distinguished and prolific families in America, the Randolphs of Virginia. His great-grandfather was Sir John Randolph (d. 1737), who was among many other things a law reporter and therefore also discussed in this book. John Randolph "the Tory" (d. 1784) was his grandfather, and his father was Edmund Randolph (d. 1813), who was governor of Virginia, United States attorney general, and secretary of state. His mother, Elizabeth Nicholas Randolph, came from a family which was very active in Virginia politics during the eighteenth and nineteenth centuries.

Peyton Randolph was born in 1779 and graduated from the College of William and Mary in 1798. On March 15, 1806, he married Maria Ward in Amelia County. She was the daughter of Benjamin and Mary Ward, and it is said that she had rejected a proposal of marriage from John Randolph of Roanoke.

Randolph acquired a reputation as a distinguished lawyer in Richmond and became active in public affairs, as was expected of a Randolph. He attained the rank of captain in the Richmond Light Infantry Blues but resigned in 1808 "on account of the reduced condition of the company." He was active in the encouragement of manufacturing in America, particularly in Richmond, in order to avoid further maritime difficulties with France and Great Britain, who were at war with each other and seizing American vessels. A letter to this effect was published in the Richmond *Enquirer* on July 22, 1808, signed by William Cabell, William Wirt, Thomas Ritchie, William Foushee, and Peyton Randolph as a committee of the Manufacturing Association.

On January 4, 1809, Randolph was appointed to the Council of State, the advisory board to the governor. It is interesting to note that this prestigious election was apparently Randolph's first success in politics; it leads one to suspect that his family and friends were behind it.

The next two and a half years were uneventful for Randolph. However, on December 26, 1811, the governor of Virginia, George William Smith, died in the disastrous burning of the Richmond Theatre. Normally the president of the Council of State would have become the acting governor, but the Council of State had not elected a president; therefore Peyton Randolph, its senior member, acted as governor. The General Assembly was always extremely sensitive as to its powers and prerogatives and took umbrage at this. The legislature annually replaced two members of the Council, and when they reconvened on January 2, 1812, one of the first things they did was vote Randolph off the Council. James Barbour was elected governor the next day. Thus was Randolph's office terminated in seven days.

Randolph was the official reporter for the Virginia Court of Appeals from 1821 to 1828. As such he published six volumes of reports.

He died in Richmond on December 26, 1828, of a pulmonary disease. His wife had predeceased him by two years, but his son Edmund lived on and became a famous attorney in California, dying in 1861.

Sources: J. Daniels, *Randolphs of Virginia* (New York, 1972), pp. xviii, 231, 289; L. G. Tyler, *Encyclopedia of Va. Biog.*, (New York, 1915) 2:47, 48; L. G. Tyler, *Hist. of Va.* (Chicago, 1924), 2:447; R. A. Brock, *Va. and Virginians* (Richmond, 1888), 1:447; *Va. Cavalcade* 3, no. 3 (1953): 43; *Cal. of Va. State Papers*, 10:3, 40; K. B. Williams, *Marriages of Amelia Co.* (Alexandria, 1964), p. 89; M. V. Smith, *Virginia, Hist. of Executives* (Washington, D.C., 1893), p. 320.

Benjamin Watkins Leigh

Philip M. Grabill, Jr.

Benjamin Watkins Leigh was born on June 18, 1781, at Gravel Hill, his family's home in Chesterfield County near Petersburg. His father, the Reverend William Leigh, had been educated at the College of William and Mary and then had studied theology at Edinburgh. His father died when he was only six, leaving him to be brought up by his mother, Elizabeth Watkins Leigh, who was well connected in Virginia society. Leigh was educated at the school of the Reverend Needler Robinson, an Episcopalian Scotsman who had succeeded the elder Leigh as rector of Dale Parish. He then matriculated at William and Mary, where a part of his course of study included St. George Tucker's law lectures. He attended these lectures during the academic year 1800–1801. He apparently felt that he had not received the full benefit of Judge Tucker's legal erudition, for he and Chapman Johnson repeated this one-year course the next academic year, having spent the summer in independent reading.

Leigh was admitted to the Petersburg bar in 1802 at the age of twenty-one. His verbal skills and ability to present a strong convincing argument became evident in his very first case. The case gained widespread publicity, when Leigh became emotionally involved in his defense of a youth accused of killing his stepfather as he beat the child's mother. His arguments, which were filled with personal feeling and sharp concise legal reasoning, were successful in gaining the boy's acquittal.

His next case was before the Supreme Court of Appeals, where his own right to practice law had been challenged because he refused to take an oath to suppress dueling, which was required of all officers of the state. After a previous ruling against him, Leigh was able to persuade the court that his adherence to principle was not prohibited by the state statute.

In 1811 Leigh was elected to the House of Delegates for two sessions. While in the legislature he served on the Courts of Justice Committee and became known as the state's leading authority on legal questions. Also during his service as a legislator, he presented resolutions on and became one of the strongest supporters of instruction of the United States senators by the legislature which elected them, advocating that the senators be required to follow the directions of the state legislature in voting on issues before Congress. This stand would later be thrown back at him in an attempt to discredit his consistency. Leigh's political views were conservative, and he was a member of the Whig party.

In 1813 Leigh moved to Richmond to pursue his private practice of law. Except for several periods of public service, he spent the rest of his life in Richmond. By the time he moved, Leigh was married for the third time. His two previous wives had been Mary Seldon Watkins, his first cousin, and Susan Colston, a niece of Chief Justice John Marshall. His third wife was Julia Wickham, daughter of John Wickham, a prominent Virginia lawyer. They lived on the corner of Clay and Tenth streets in a house built for Julia's grandfather, Dr. James McClurg.

In 1818 Leigh wrote a series of letters to the Richmond *Enquirer*, one of the most powerful newspapers in the South. In the letters, which he wrote under the signature of "Algernon Sidney," Leigh expounded on the value of civil liberty and the threat of the federal government's encroachment upon it. He said: "I can yet never be indifferent to great questions of right that directly affect the peace, the honor, and the Constitution of my country. . . . Liberty is not of spontaneous growth in any soil or clime, and he is deaf to the voice of experience, who deems it that hardy plant, which will flourish ever after it has taken root, without continual pains and cultivation." In another of the letters Leigh stated that neither the president nor the Congress nor the two combined had the power to declare martial law in this country. Leigh also used the letters to denounce the military career of General Andrew Jackson, a person for whom he would entertain a strong dissatisfaction throughout all of his years of public service.

In 1819 the Virginia legislature chose Leigh to supervise the important task of collecting and revising the laws of the state. Leigh, along with Hening and Munford, prepared the Revised Code of 1819. In 1822 the Commonwealth of Virginia again called on Leigh to perform another service of great significance. Kentucky had been formed from part of Virginia, and Virginia still claimed legal title under Kentucky law to some of these lands. However, the Kentucky legislature passed a law, popularly known as the "occupying claimants law," which would have annulled Virginia's title to this land. The Virginia General Assembly appointed Leigh as commissioner to Kentucky to try to persuade that state to amend its law. The Kentucky legislature heard Leigh's arguments and rejected his proposals, but it did appoint Henry Clay as commissioner to negotiate with him. These two statesmen reached an agreement whereby the states would submit to an impartial board of arbitration. But the Virginia Senate refused to enter the arbitration, thus ending the negotiations. Leigh returned home very disappointed that his state had rejected what he termed his "best efforts at public service."

Leigh again returned to private life and the practice of law until 1829. The Virginia Supreme Court of Appeals commissioned him as a reporter to compile opinions of the court, which he did until 1841, completing twelve volumes of court decisions.

Also in the same year, 1829, Leigh was selected to participate in the state Constitutional Convention of 1829–30. The citizens of the western part of the state felt that their power to participate in state government was weakened by the existing laws on suffrage, which was based on the amount of taxation paid. The western counties were not as wealthy as those in the east. A convention was called to deal with this and other areas of dissatisfaction with the constitution. Although Leigh lived in Richmond, his native county of

Chesterfield chose him to represent it at the convention. It has been said by many that in this forum, Leigh reached the height of his political career. He was acclaimed as the single most influential participant in the convention. This is no small tribute when one reads the list of representatives, which included John Randolph of Roanoke, Madison, Monroe, Marshall, Tyler, and the leader of Leigh's western opponents, Chapman Johnson, one of his closest friends.

The eastern delegation to the convention sought a leader who was young, active, and eager for combat. They wanted a person never fatigued, never disheartened, never disposed to reject the post of honor, no matter how dangerous it might be. They chose Benjamin Watkins Leigh. In his sketches of the convention, Hugh R. Pleasants offers us a picture of the man who was to lead the eastern forces. Leigh was forty-eight and well seasoned, with no superior at the Virginia bar. He was better acquainted with the history of Virginia legislation than any other delegate. "He was a small man, uncommonly well made, very graceful with a hand that would have famed a study for Kneller, eyes of uncommon brilliancy, a forehead of striking beauty, hair as black as the wings of a raven, and glossy and fine as a lady's, and features which but for a nose that was somewhat too short would have been classically handsome." Leigh wore a thick sole on one shoe to compensate for a short leg caused by an earlier break.

On the voting issue, Leigh felt that those who paid the most in taxes should have the most power in conducting the operation of government. While the western delegation favored representation based purely on the number of free citizens of a district, Leigh supported representation based on tax revenue received from the district plus the number of citizens. Leigh attacked the pure numbers system on the grounds that there were many poverty-stricken free whites in the west doing work performed by Negro slaves in the east. It would be unwise to place voting strength in these illiterate whites who contributed no revenue for state use. Although he was not successful on his proposals, he achieved a compromise whereby the voting power was allocated on a numerical basis with slaves counting three-fifths, leaving much strength in the east.

In 1830 he represented Henrico County in the House of Delegates, and in 1833 Leigh was called upon by the legislature to serve as a commissioner to South Carolina. That state had been protesting federal taxation and was attempting to gain support for a taxation nullification or a refusal to pay federal taxes. Although Virginia was not happy with the federal tax structure, it knew the dangerous potential of such a drastic proposal. The state relied on Leigh to attempt to dissuade the South Carolina legislature from following this course of action. He addressed the group and worked with others to influence successfully the governing body to soften their attack. This was one of the very few times Leigh found himself on the same side of a political issue with Andrew Jackson.

Leigh was a longtime political opponent of Jackson. He viewed him as incompetent for the office of president and attacked his increased wielding of executive power. A burning issue at this time was the existence of the Bank of the United States. Jackson opposed it, and when his efforts to influence Congress to terminate its charter failed, he ordered the secretary of the Treasury to begin a gradual withdrawal of public funds from the bank. The state of Virginia abhorred this action, and the General Assembly instructed the United States senators from Virginia, to support resolutions to censure the president for abusing his power. Senator William C. Rives, a Democrat, refused to follow the instruction and resigned. Because of his strong stand against Jackson and his actions, Leigh was chosen by the legislature to replace Rives; he took his place as senator on March 5, 1834, as a member of the Whig party. Leigh actually had mixed feelings on the existence of the national bank. He felt that there was no legal basis for such an institution, but that it performed a service to the country so great in value as to outweigh the legal question. On one matter Leigh was certain: Andrew Jackson had exceeded his legal and constitutional power as president by ordering the withdrawal of public funds from the bank. On several occasions in the United States Senate, Leigh spoke in support of resolutions condemning Jackson and demanding the restoration of the deposits in the bank. In one of his speeches he denounced Jackson as a tyrant who had "presumption . . . which no monarch since the days of Henry VIII ever claimed before."

Leigh's partial term in the Senate expired in 1835, and he returned home to campaign against very strong opposition to his reelection. The western part of the state still remembered the convention where he opposed their proposals. Leigh was reelected by a majority of two votes in the Virginia Senate.

When Leigh returned for the next session of Congress, Senator Thomas Hart Benton, a supporter of Jackson from Missouri, introduced a resolution to expunge from the Senate Journal the resolutions condemning Jackson for his activities in regard to the bank. The Virginia legislature had undergone a major change and now instructed Leigh and Senator John Tyler to support Benton's resolution. Senator Tyler refused to follow the instructions and resigned. Leigh also refused to follow the instructions, but he refused to resign. He spoke against Benton's resolution and helped to defeat it. Leigh faced sharp criticism, especially because he had been the leading supporter of the instruction doctrine while in the Virginia legislature. He wrote a long letter to the General Assembly stating that although he believed in the doctrine, he had always maintained that the legislature did not have the authority to instruct a senator to perform an act inconsistent with the Constitution. In 1836 Leigh resigned from the Senate for "personal reasons" and returned to Richmond and to private life for the remainder of his days. Leigh had a brilliant intellect and was greatly admired as a politician and as an orator. However, he was not in the slightest concerned to enhance his personal fame or popularity; he preferred the satisfaction of a quiet conscience and intellectual consistency to the applause of the populace. Therefore he accepted public office, but he never sought it wholeheartedly as one must to attain political heights.

The legal scholarship of Leigh consisted of his work on the Revised Code of 1819, his twelve volumes of reports, and a note on the Virginia law of descents which was published long after his death in the *Virginia Law Journal,* 9 (1885): pp. 199–208. His major literary contributions are his political speeches and pamphlets:

Proceedings of the Legislature of Va. in Support of the Right of State Legislators to Instruct Their Senators in Congress, Lexington, Ky., 1812.

Substitute . . . on the Subject of the Right of the State Legislatures to Instruct Their Senators, [Richmond, 1812].

Speech . . . on the Subject of the Military Land Claims Delivered Before the Legislature of Ky. on 17th May 1822, [1822?].

Substitute . . . on the Subject of a Convention, Richmond, 1824.

The Letters of Algernon Sydney in Defense of Civil Liberty and Against the Encroachments of Military Despotism . . . 1818–19, Richmond, 1830.

Essays on the American System, Philadelphia, 1831.

The Letter of Appomattox . . . on the Subject of the Abolition of Slavery, Richmond, 1832.

Speech . . . on the Motion That the President's Protest . . . Should Not Be Received, Washington, D.C., 1834.

Speeches . . . on the Removal of the Deposits and on the Bill to Extend the Charter of the Bank, Washington, D.C., 1834.

Speech of Mr. Leigh in Reply to Mr. Wright . . . on Mr. Webster's Motion to Renew the Charter of the Bank, Richmond, [1834].

Speech . . . on Mr. Benton's Motion to Expunge from the Journal of the Senate, [2 editions], Washington, D.C., 1836.

Speech . . . of the Reception of Certain Memorials . . . to Abolish Slavery Within the District of Columbia, [Washington, 1836].

Letter from B. W. Leigh to the General Assembly of Va. on Expunging from the Journal of the Senate the Resolution of March 28th, 1834, [Washington, D.C. (?), 1836].

Leigh was honored in 1835 with a doctorate in laws from William and Mary. He refused reappointment as official law reporter for Virginia in 1842 and was succeeded by Conway Robinson. He died on February 2, 1849, in Richmond and was buried in Shockoe Cemetery. He was survived by numerous children, one of whom was married to Robinson.

Sources: DAB, s.v. "Leigh, Benjamin Watkins"; *Biog. Directory of the Am. Congress* (Washington, D.C., 1971), p. 1281; E. J. Smith, "B. W. Leigh" *Branch Hist. Papers* 1 (1904): 286–89; Munford's *Reports*, 1:468; *Richmond Portraits* (Richmond, 1949), p. 107; A. W. Weddell, *Portraiture in the Va. Hist. Soc.* (Richmond, 1945), pp. 64, 65; Swem and Williams, *Register of the Genl. Assembly*, pp. 81, 83, 129, 245; H. B. Grigsby, *Va. Convention of 1829–30* (New York, 1969), pp. 78 ff.; *Va. Hist. Reg.* 2 (1849): 104–7; Leigh papers in Va. Hist. Soc.; *Southern Literary Messenger* 17 (1851): 123–27, 147–54; *Speech of J. T. Brown upon the Election of a Senator* [Leigh] (Richmond, 1835); B. E. Steiner, "Prelude to Conservatism, 1781–1822," M.A. thesis, U. Va., 1959.

Conway Robinson

Richard A. Claybrook, Jr.

Conway Robinson was born in Richmond on September 15, 1805. His father was John Robinson, clerk of the Henrico circuit court, and his mother was Agnes Conway Moncure Robinson. The Robinson family lived in a town house called Catalpa Hall on the east side of Sixth Street between Main and Franklin, and they had a house in the country, Poplar Vale, on land that is now known as Byrd Park.

Conway Robinson attended Chiles Terrill's school near Capitol Square, his only formal education. At the age of thirteen, he became an assistant to Thomas C. Howard, clerk of two of the local courts of Richmond. He served with Howard for six years; then in 1824 the two courts were separated, and Robinson became clerk of the more important one, serving in that capacity for the next three years. In 1826 he in addition became assistant clerk of the General Court, being named full clerk in 1828. Robinson was admitted to the Richmond bar in 1827, at the age of twenty-one. He resigned his clerkship in 1831 in order to devote all his time to his growing law practice.

Conway Robinson was a man of diverse interests, one of the most important of which was historical research. He assisted in 1831 in the founding of the Virginia Historical Society and served as the society's first treasurer. He later served as chairman of the executive committee and vice-president of the society. John Selden wrote that Robinson presented the society "from time to time, with documents, foreign and domestic, of the highest value, contributed to enrich its gallery with historical portraits, and penned for its archives numerous learned and instructive treatises."

On July 14, 1836, he married Mary Susan Selden Leigh, daughter of Benjamin Watkins Leigh. She was, according to

Selden, "a lady pious in soul, of strong and cultivated intelligence, and graced with every charm of disposition, of person, and of manner." The Robinsons had at least seven children, five of whom survived their father, as did his wife. During the years they lived in Richmond, the Robinsons at first rented a house on the north side of Broad Street between Ninth and Tenth streets. About 1842, they bought a house on Seventh Street between Clay and Leigh streets, and in 1849 or 1850 they built a large new home next door.

In 1836 Conway Robinson became the second president of the Richmond, Fredericksburg, and Potomac Railroad Company, which was in financial trouble at the time. Within seven months of his acceptance of the presidency, the line was completed and operating to Fredericksburg. In November 1838 Robinson withdrew from the presidency over the objections of the railroad's stockholders, but he remained the company's legal adviser, participating in one capacity or another in all litigation of importance with which it was connected.

Robinson was admitted to practice before the United States Supreme Court in 1839. He was a close friend of then Chief Justice Roger Taney and had been a social friend of the late Chief Justice John Marshall.

Robinson succeeded his father-in-law, Benjamin Watkins Leigh, as reporter to the Virginia Supreme Court of Appeals on May 10, 1842, when Leigh declined reappointment. He published two volumes known as *Robinson's Virginia Reports*, volumes forty and forty-one of the Virginia Reporter System. The first volume contained in its preface much important information concerning the earlier judicial system of Virginia, including a brief history of the appellate system in the state and an outline of the succession of reporters to the Court of Appeals to that time. Selden praised Robinson's *Reports* as distinguished for thoroughness and felicity of execution. Robinson resigned as reporter on April 1, 1844, to devote more time to other phases of his career.

In February 1846 Robinson was selected by the General Assembly along with John M. Patton, Sr., to revise the civil code of Virginia, and in March 1847 he and Patton were selected to revise the state criminal code. Their proposals, which were contained in five volumes, were enacted in August 1849 and went into effect July 1, 1850. The new code was designed to reconcile the contradictions and incongruities of the local law and to eliminate the defects, without destroying the substance, of the common law system. In the process of preparing the new code, Robinson researched the jurisprudence of England and other state codes in this country. He served as a member of the General Assembly during its 1852 session and during that "protracted session" contributed to the adaptation of the new code to the requirements of the new state constitution of 1851.

From 1849 to 1853, except during the 1852 General Assembly session, Robinson served (without salary) as a member of the Richmond City Council. Selden credits him with spearheading the advances during that period in municipal government, particularly in respect to public education, gas, water, streets, parks, and the improvement of the Capitol Square. During his tenure, Monroe Park, Gamble's Hill Park, and Libby Hill Park were established, and other parks were planned. Robinson also worked to establish the Athenaeum as a center for such cultural activities as the Richmond Library and the Virginia Historical Society.

In 1853 Robinson traveled to England on a vacation and collected many valuable historical documents relating to Virginia and to colonial America. During this trip he established permanent friendships with many distinguished persons.

In the summer of 1858, in order to have access to more extensive libraries, such as the Library of Congress, Robinson moved to Washington, D.C. He built a home called The Vineyard adjoining the Soldier's Home and overlooking the Potomac River across to Virginia. Thus his legal writing, which was no longer limited to Virginia, could be more easily pursued. However, Robinson maintained a law partnership in Richmond with James Alfred Jones and frequently returned to argue cases in the Court of Appeals, which, in that day, had a very exclusive bar. In fact, as few as ten or twelve lawyers did practically all the practice of the Court of Appeals at that time. Robinson's law practice after 1858, nevertheless, was carried on mainly before the United States Supreme Court.

He did not appear in the Court from 1861 to 1866, when the "test-oath" of loyalty to the Union was required of advocates, because he refused to subscribe to it. Selden describes Robinson as "anguished" by the Civil War. "He had loved Virginia, but he had looked with patriotic attachment upon the Union, and upon each of the parts of which it was composed." Three of his sons fought for the Confederacy, and two were killed in action. Robinson resumed his large and lucrative practice before the Virginia Supreme Court of Appeals and the United States Supreme Court in 1866. He continued to practice before the Virginia court until 1878 and before the latter court until 1883.

Judge George L. Christian describes Robinson as "quite tall, a man of most benign countenance, of distinguished appearance, and attractive manners." Selden wrote that he was "singularly handsome" and possessed "industry, a faculty of analysis, and ability and passion for continuous investigation and research." In addition to being among the most eminent and admired practitioners of the law, Robinson was among the most scholarly, and he was also one of the most prolific legal writers produced by Virginia. His publications reflect clearly his professional progress. His first book was a second edition of his father's *Collection of the Most Useful and Approved Forms,* which was published in 1826 while he was a clerk of court.

At the outset of his practice, Robinson wrote a three-volume work, *Practice in the Courts of Law and Equity in Virginia* (1832–39). The significance of this work was described by one of his contemporaries, Alexander H. Sands, who was also a legal writer and lawyer of note. "These works gave Mr. Robinson a hold upon the legal fraternity rarely secured in Virginia. For more than the third of a century they were quoted and relied on as authority in the inferior, superior and supreme courts of the State. They contained discussions of a practical character to which no other treatises had then been devoted, and they were almost free from error. In a practice extended now over thirty years, in their almost daily use, frequently citing them himself and witnessing their citation by others, the writer of this notice has never found an error of an importance in these volumes. Similar testimony is furnished by others. For faultless accuracy and clear and concise statement of legal principles the first two volumes of Mr. Robinson's *Practice* are unrivaled among law books published in this country." After the publication of his general encyclopedia of practice beginning in 1854, this Virginia work became known as "Robinson's Old *Practice*."

By 1841 the second edition of his father's book of Virginia legal forms was out of print so he published in that year under his own name *Forms Adapted to the Practice in Virginia*, Volume I. This work was compiled as a supplement to the first volume of his *Practice in Virginia*. Additional volumes were planned to provide forms for equity, probate, and criminal practice, but Robinson never got around to them.

In 1840 Robinson wrote an article entitled "Slavery and the Constitution," which was published in the *Southern Literary Messenger*, vol. 6, pp. 89–106, and also printed separately as *An Essay upon the Constitutional Rights as to Slave Property*.

His next publications were his two volumes of *Virginia Reports*. These cover the period 1842 to 1844 and appeared in 1843 and 1844. Both volumes have prefaces which discuss the history of the Virginia system of courts, the *Virginia Reports* and the laws concerning them, and the backlog of cases clogging the Supreme Court of Appeals.

Robinson was very interested in the history of Virginia, and in addition to being one of the organizers of the Virginia Historical Society, he did much research and note taking in various archives. His first publication in this area was in 1845 in the *Southern Literary Messenger*, vol. 11, p. 49, a letter describing some materials for the colonial history of Virginia which he had come across. His major historical contribution was his *Account of Discoveries in the West Until 1519, and of Voyages to*

and Along the Atlantic Coast of North America, from 1520 to 1573
(Richmond, 1848), which was prepared for the Virginia
Historical Society.

The notes that Robinson made in his lifetime have been the
subject of editing by later historians after his death. The larger
work is *Abstract of the Proceedings of the Virginia Company of
London, 1619–1624, Prepared from the Records in the Library of
Congress by Conway Robinson*, edited by R. A. Brock, *Collections
of the Virginia Historical Society*, n.s., vols. 7, 8 (1888, 1889). Of
more importance are the brief notes he made from the General
Court records in Richmond before the state archives were
destroyed by fire in 1865. These notes have been printed in part
in the *Virginia Magazine of History and Biography*, vols. 3–5, 8, 9,
10, 13, 14, and in H. R. McIlwaine, *Minutes of the Council
and General Court of Colonial Virginia* (1924). In 1877 he presented
an article to the recently established *Virginia Law Journal*, "Of
Lawyers in Virginia between 1707 and 1737," vol. 1, pp.
191–96. This consisted of brief sketches of Stevens Thomson,
John Holloway, William Hopkins, and Sir John Randolph.

Shortly after resigning in 1844 as the Virginia law reporter,
Conway Robinson became involved in legislative reform. He
and John Mercer Patton, Sr., were appointed the official
revisors of the Code of Virginia. They published from 1847 to
1849 their annotated proposals, *Report of the Revisors*, in five
installments. This was the original version of the Code of
1849. After the General Assembly had discussed, amended,
and enacted the new code, it was officially issued by Patton
and Robinson, introduced by a scholarly essay on the history of
the codes of Virginia.

In 1850 there was a movement for constitutional reform in
the Commonwealth. In this year Robinson published his
Views of the Constitution of Virginia. Here he opposed the
attempts to amend the state constitution; he offered himself
as a representative to the forthcoming convention but was not
elected.

Robinson's major literary accomplishment appeared in seven
substantial volumes from 1854 to 1874, his *Practice in the Courts*

of Justice in England and the United States. Sands said that with but one exception this work was "the largest body of accurate law yet published in this country. Many of these volumes secured the highest commendation from distinguished sources in Great Britain, and with one accord the legal journals of this country spoke of them in the highest terms of praise."

His interests in politics and in the Richmond, Fredericksburg, and Potomac Railroad continued in his later days. His concern for politics resulted in a series of short but erudite newspaper articles in 1876:

"Neither the Attorney General nor the Secretary of War nor the President of the United States Can Authorize an Act Which the Law Makes Punishable by Fine and Imprisonment at Hard Labor, and by Disqualification from Holding Office." Boston *Post*, Sept. 14, 1876; Albany *Argus*, Sept. 15, 1876; Washington *Sentinel*, Sept. 16, 1876.

"As to the Effect of Voting for a Person as Elector of President and Vice President, When Such Person Holds an Office of Trust or Profit Under the United States." Washington, D.C., *Sentinel*, Dec. 2, 1876.

"Of Corrupt Officers; Conspirators Aiming by Fraud and Force to Defeat the Voice of the People in Elections and to Overthrow Constitutional Government." Washington, D.C., *Union*, Dec. 7, 1876; Washington, D.C. *Sentinel*, Dec. 9, 1876.

"Impeaching Officers of the United States." Washington, D.C., *Union*, Dec. 9, 1876.

"Of the Power Which the Framers of the Constitution Would Not Give the Senate—and Did Give the House of Representatives—to Choose a President." Washington, D.C., *Union*, Dec. 14, 1876.

In 1878 he published two pamphlets on behalf of the railroad with which he had long been associated: *Views of Conway Robinson upon Questions Before an Adjourned Meeting of the Stockholders in the R., F., & P. RR. Co. on the 3rd Day of April, 1878,* and *Communication of Aug. 7, 1878, from Conway Robinson, to Moncure Robinson and Thomas A. Biddle, Proxies for*

Stockholders in the R. F. & P. RR. Co. Residing in Great Britain and Pennsylvania.

Conway Robinson's last years were spent writing legal history. In 1882 he published the first volume of his *History of the High Court of Chancery and Other Institutions of England.* The 1,215 pages of this book cover the subject from Roman times to the death of Henry VIII in 1547; he had almost completed the second volume, which would have continued the history down to 1689, the accession of William and Mary, but death intervened. He died of pneumonia on January 30, 1884, in Philadelphia. He was buried in Hollywood Cemetery in Richmond, and his library and papers were given to the Virginia Historical Society. Both are indeed appropriate places for Conway Robinson's physical and literary remains.

Sources: DAB, s.v. "Robinson, Conway"; *Va. L. Journ.* 8 (1884): 257–66; *Va. L. Reg.* 1 (1896): 60, 61, 631–46, and 14 (1909): 661–62; *Albany Law Journ.* 29 (1884): 165, 166; *Richmond Portraits* (Richmond, 1949), pp. 175–77; A. W. Weddell, *Portraiture*, pp. 96, 97; Swem and Williams, *Register of the General Assembly*, p. 173; *Va. Mag. Hist. Biog.* 78 (1970): 259–67; conversation with Lee Shepard.

Peachy Ridgway Grattan

Thomas M. Blaylock

Peachy Ridgway Grattan was born on November 7, 1801, at his family's estate, Contentment, located near Mount Crawford in Rockingham County. In 1827 he married Jane Elvira Ferguson. They had five children, one of whom, George Gilmer Grattan, was killed at the battle of Seven Pines. One of Grattan's sisters was married to George R. Gilmer, a congressman from Georgia, and one of his nephews, G. G. Grattan, became a judge in Rockingham County.

In 1835 at the age of thirty-four, Grattan moved to Richmond, and there he resided and practiced law with great success for the rest of his long life. On April 9, 1844, he was unanimously appointed reporter of the Virginia Supreme Court of Appeals in the place of Conway Robinson, who had resigned several days before. Grattan remained the official reporter until his death in 1881. It is interesting to note that he retained this position before, during, and after the Confederacy and Reconstruction. This alone must be regarded as a personal tribute to his integrity and to his competence.

Politics as well as law was of interest to Peachy Grattan. The first glimpse of his political views that we get is from his apparent support of the South Carolina Nullification Ordinance of 1832 even though the great majority of his neighbors of Rockingham County were strongly opposed to it.

Three years after his arrival in Richmond, in 1838, Grattan was elected to the Board of Managers of the Virginia Branch of the American Colonization Society, and he served as an active member until at least 1859. This organization was active in helping freed blacks to relocate and begin new lives in Liberia. The Virginia branch was founded in 1823 with John Marshall as its president. Marshall held that office until his death in 1835; he was succeeded by John Tyler, who was president when Grattan was first made a manager.

Grattan was a member of the Richmond City Council from 1857 to the end of the War Between the States. His most significant service to the city appears to have been his participation in the drafting of a new city charter in 1861 and in the lobbying necessary to get it passed by the General Assembly. In 1865 he was elected to represent the city in the Virginia House of Delegates. Grattan's political life was cut short by the military government during Reconstruction, and he did not return to politics afterwards.

The most important of Grattan's publications are his thirty-three volumes of the *Virginia Reports*, which cover the period 1844 to 1880. This series of reports is by far the longest in Virginia. Grattan only rarely interjected anything of his own into these official publications. There is, however, a three-page preface to volume eight, which notes the reorganization of the courts in 1851. He seems uneasy over the change to a popularly elected judiciary but consoles himself with a vague religious fatalism. The same attitude is present in his sorrowful note on the Capitol Disaster of April 27, 1870, which is in volume nineteen at pages 673 to 676. On this date the courtroom was packed with spectators to hear the decision of the Court of Appeals in the *Richmond Mayoralty Case*, which would determine whether the carpetbaggers would retain control of the city government. The floor, gallery, and ceiling of the courtroom collapsed into the chamber of the House of Delegates below, killing fifty-eight persons and seriously injuring many more.

On June 2, 1857, Grattan delivered a speech about slavery to the General Assembly of the Presbyterian Church at a meeting in Cleveland, Ohio. In this speech he demonstrated his belief that the status quo must be maintained; the slaves could not be emancipated because they would be impoverished and homeless with no one to provide for them. He was skeptical of the attempts to return the slaves to Africa, noting the enormous expense which would make the project impossible. During his speech he made the comparison of a master turning out his slaves to that of a father who would send his children away from home before they were equipped with the knowledge and maturity to take care of themselves. Grattan felt that the slaves had no right to liberty at that time but that they did have a right to protection from their masters and from themselves. Of the effect of Northern condemnation of slavery he had no doubt. "One thing is clear to my mind beyond all cavil or question, and that is, that the further agitation of this subject can produce nothing but evil; evil to the master, greater evil to the slave; evil to the North and to the South; evil to the country and to the Church; evil which will be felt in all time, and in eternity." This speech was published in Richmond in 1857, four years before the Civil War began.

In 1861 Grattan was busy attending to the affairs of the city of Richmond. In this year he published a fourteen-page tract, *Letter, on the Constitutional Power of the General Assembly to Extend the Boundaries of the City of Richmond, and on the Propriety of the Application* (Richmond, 1861).

He also wrote two articles for the *Virginia Law Journal*: "Jurisdiction of Common Law Courts in Attachments," 1 (1877): 587-91, and "War Interest on the State Debt," 2, (1878): 65-72. Both were scholarly contributions to legal problems of the day.

Sometime after 1865 Grattan moved to Ashland and commuted to Richmond. He died in Ashland on September 8, 1881, and was buried in Richmond in Hollywood Cemetery. He was a very religious and a rigidly conscientious man, and he was highly respected as a lawyer.

Sources: L. H. Manarin, *Richmond at War* (Chapel Hill, N.C., 1966), pp. 16, 74, 629; *Va. Mag. Hist. Biog.* 24 (1916): 222; *Wm. & Mary Qtly.*, 1st ser. 17 (1908): 142; J. W. Wayland, *Men of Mark* (Staunton, 1943), p. 402; J. W. Wayland, *Hist. of Rockingham Co.* (Dayton, Va., 1912), pp. 117, 322; *Va. Law Journ.* 5 (1881): 659, 725; *Va. Law Reg.* 14 (1909): 739, 740; MS minute book of Am. Colonization Soc. in Va. Hist. Soc.; Swem and Williams, *Reg. of the General Assembly*, p. 189.

Sir John Randolph

R. Earl Nance

John Randolph was born in 1693 in Henrico County, the sixth son of William and Mary Isham Randolph. William Randolph founded one of the most celebrated families in eighteenth-century Virginia. He was wealthy and politically active as a justice of the peace and Speaker of the House of Burgesses, among other offices. Thus John Randolph grew up in an intellectual and political setting. As was the custom of the affluent colonial families, he received his early education at home under a tutor; his tutor was a clergyman, possibly a Huguenot refugee.

Randolph furthered his education at the College of William and Mary before being admitted on May 17, 1715, to Gray's Inn in London. He studied law for two and a half years in an English lawyer's office and was called to the bar on November 25, 1717. He soon returned to Virginia and began the practice of law in Williamsburg. On April 28, 1718, at the age of twenty-five he was appointed clerk of the House of Burgesses. He held his clerkship until 1734. He also held the office of king's attorney.

Randolph's success in business affairs is attested to by his appointment as the representative of Virginia in 1728 to go to England and petition the House of Commons in regard to the tobacco trade. He completed his mission with success, and the offensive clause of an Act of Parliament was repealed. He was also commissioned to attend to several matters of financial concern to the College of William and Mary. Randolph returned to Virginia and to his flourishing law practice in October 1728. It was then that he began keeping notes of the cases which he argued before the General Court, or perhaps we should say that this is when his surviving reports began. In 1732 Randolph was again called upon to represent the interests of colonial Virginia in London. Again the problem involved tobacco, the major financial concern of the colony. An additional tax on Virginia tobacco was threatened, and a system of warehouses was proposed in order to reduce smuggling and other frauds upon the existing system. The unsuccessful Excise Bill of 1733 was a compromise on these fiscal matters, but the colonials did not get what they wanted. Randolph was recognized as a man who could not be ignored and was rewarded with a knighthood; he was the only colonial Virginian ever to be so honored.

Sir John Randolph soon returned home whereupon his political skill was rewarded by his election to the House of Burgesses to represent the College of William and Mary. In 1734 he was made treasurer of the colony and Speaker of the House of Burgesses. His popularity and prestige continued, and in November 1736 he was elected the first recorder of the newly incorporated Borough of Norfolk. The choice of Sir John for this position was evidently to attach his personal fame to the new city, for from the beginning he exercised the office through a deputy, David Osheoll.

Sir John Randolph's reports cover the period October 1729 to April 1732. They consist of Randolph's own arguments, much shorter accounts of his opponent's points, and finally how the judges voted. In this period the judges of the General Court, the highest court in colonial Virginia, never gave reasons for their decisions. One can assume, however, that they were persuaded by the arguments of the lawyers. The judges of the eighteenth century were all educated gentlemen and many had studied law. In any case, we are fortunate to have the legal arguments of Sir John Randolph because he was the most highly respected lawyer of his day in Virginia. These reports, which existed only in manuscript, were published by R. T. Barton in 1909.

Randolph published two tracts on the subject of the Virginia tobacco trade. These were a part of his lobbying activities in London on behalf of the colonial government. These two pamphlets were published as *The Case of the Planters of Tobacco in Virginia; To Which Is Added a Vindication of the Said Representation*, London, 1733. Two examples of his eloquence as a speaker can be found in the *Journals of the House of Burgesses, 1727-1740*, pp. 175-76, 239-42. The first of these was printed separately in 1734, and the latter part of the second, a speech on the constitution of Virginia in 1736, was reproduced in *English Historical Documents*, vol. 9, pp. 268-71. Sir John Randolph wrote sketches of two of his contemporaries, John Holloway and William Hopkins, in his Breviate Book; these were published in 1835 in the *Southern Literary Messenger*, vol. 1, pp. 353-54.

Sir John Randolph was married to Susanna Beverley. They had four children: John "the Tory," a colonial attorney general; Peyton, who was president of the Continental Congress; Beverley; and Mary. Sir John's health began to deteriorate in 1736, and he died on March 22, 1737, in Williamsburg. He was buried in the chapel of William and Mary.

Sources: R. T. Barton, *Va. Colonial Decisions* (Boston, 1909), 1: 226-37; J. Daniels, *Randolphs of Virginia* (New York, 1972), pp. x, xviii, 43-52; H. J. Eckenrode, *Randolphs* (New York, 1946), pp. 44-51; *DAB*, s.v. "Randolph, Sir John"; *Va. L. Jour.* 1 (1877): 193-96; *Va. Hist. Reg.* 4 (1851): 138-41; *Va. Mag. Hist. Biog.* 32 (1924): 136-41, 36 (1928): 376-81, 78 (1970): 199-201; *So. Atl. Qtly.* 28 (1929): 281-92.

Edward Barradall

R. Earl Nance

Edward Barradall, one of the most prominent attorneys in Virginia in the first half of the eighteenth century, is best remembered for his *Cases Adjudged in the General Court of Virginia from April 1733 to October 1741* which was edited by R. T. Barton in 1909.

Barradall's parents are thought to have been Henry and Catherine Blumfield Barradall; this conjecture is based upon the fact that in the English Faculty Office Marriage Licenses there is an entry of a marriage license dated June 6, 1696, issued to Henry Barradall and Catherine Blumfield; since Edward was born in 1704 and had two brothers, Henry and Blumfield, the inference is very strong that Henry and Catherine Blumfield Barradall were indeed Edward's parents.

Barradall was educated in England and called to the bar at the Inner Temple. He emigrated to Virginia and began practicing in Williamsburg sometime before 1730. He enjoyed a large practice and became legal adviser to Lord Fairfax, proprietor of the Northern Neck of Virginia. Barradall later drafted the act for the quieting of title to land in the colony which was necessitated by controversy over the ownership of land in the Northern Neck.

The year 1736 marked a turning point in Barradall's career. Early in that year, on January 5, he married Sarah Fitzhugh, the youngest daughter of William Fitzhugh, a prominent attorney and judge of the Vice Admiralty Court. On November 30 of that year, Barradall was named mayor of Williamsburg; the December 3 issue of the *Virginia Gazette* described this appointment: "Last Tuesday being St. Andrew's Day, the Mayor and Aldermen of this city met at the usual Place in order to choose their Mayor, where Mayor Abraham Nicholas resigned his Mayoralty, and Mr. Barradall was immediately invested with authority. The new Mayor gave a handsome Entertainment to the Aldermen and Common-Council Men, and the Festival was celebrated with a general joy."

The competence Barradall exhibited as mayor and his increasing reputation as a lawyer among the gentry who frequented Williamsburg led to his appointment as attorney general for the colony in November 1737, along with his appointment as judge of the Vice Admiralty Court and representative of the College of William and Mary in the Virginia House of Burgesses; in each of these offices he succeeded John Clayton, who had died on November 18, 1737. Barradall retained these offices until his death in 1743. While occupying them, Barradall is credited with having sponsored several significant bills, the most notable being one to ease the harmful effects caused by the shipping of convicts to Virginia and allowing them to settle in the Northern Neck. In response to the mounting crime wave in the area, Barradall in 1740 drew up legislation which filled Virginia's quota for troops in the war against the Spaniards in America with these convicts. In the language of the act, since " 'there are in every county within this colony able-bodied persons fit to serve his majesty who follow no lawful calling or employment;' wherefore the county courts were directed to impress that kind of cannon fodder to make up Virginia's quota, carefully excepting, however, 'any person . . . who hath any vote in the election of a burgess or burgesses to serve in the general assembly of this colony or who is or shall be an indented or bought servant.' " One observer notes that the plan was "simple but cynical," and "effective beyond its contemplation"; this device was a model for similar plans throughout the English colonies. Barradall also was authorized to issue letters of marque to vessels to seize Spanish ships and subjects (and to receive a percentage of the prize) as one of his duties as judge of the Vice Admiralty Court.

The Barradall name, as a result of Edward's forceful success at the bar, was said to be "another name for one learned in the law—a name which for a long time was a terror to the young applicant for a license to practice law, and before which even a Pendleton trembled at his examination."

Barradall's reports are notes of judicial decisions during the time he was practicing in Virginia. H.W.H. Knott states: "Great care is evinced in the statements of material facts and the exact points decided." "There are no head notes"; further, the General Court never delivered written opinions, and there were invariably no stated reasons for the decisions, nor were the arguments dealt with adequately. Nevertheless, "the reports are very instructive, dealing with construction of wills or deeds relating to land, actions of trespass involving the ownership of real estate, actions of detinue relative to ownership of slaves, and occasional suits for slander, thus giving a vivid picture of the course of litigation in the early days of the colony." The cases reported by Barradall are often the same as those reported by Sir John Randolph; Randolph and Barradall were often opposed to each other in court during Randolph's later years. Barradall practiced law in Randolph's shadow, and this is also true of his style in court. Barton comments that "Barradall's style in the argument of cases is more labored and less interesting than that of Randolph. There is greater display of learning, and more evidence of preparation and research [on Barradall's part], but it can readily be seen that Randolph was the superior advocate." The quality and thoroughness of Barradall's reports are superior to those of Randolph; "they are rather more liberal in noting the views of Randolph than the latter seems to have been of the positions taken in the arguments by his opponents." Barradall's reports contain portions of over ninety cases, while Randolph's reports contain only about forty cases.

Barradall's reports, as well as Randolph's, have been described by Barton as the "little fountains to be sought chiefly by those who will always seek the sources, no matter how wide may be the stream." In cases where both colonial and English law were involved, English law was followed generally but modified by local statutes and custom. Since local custom permeated nearly every area of law and more and more cases of "mixed complexion were likely to arise," it became "a matter of concern to the busy lawyer to have at hand the decisions of the General Court, the highest in the colony, and the chief tribunal of both original and appellate jurisdiction." These reports constitute the chief part of the few reported cases of the colonial Virginia era, but from these "little fountains" flow the main stream of Virginia law today. To Barradall, the legal profession owes continuing gratitude for his energy, dedication, and commitment. Death overtook Barradall at the age of thirty-nine on June 19, 1743, while he was dutifully engaged in his offices of attorney general, judge of the Vice Admiralty Court, member of the House of Burgesses, and vestryman of Bruton Parish Church in Williamsburg.

Sources: Barton, *Va. Colonial Decisions*, 1: 243–48; *DAB*, s.v. "Barradall, Edward"; W. Meade, *Old Churches* (Philadelphia, 1931), 1: 198, 199; *Va. Mag. Hist. Biog.* 14 (1906): 5, 6, 30 (1922): 256; *Va. Hist. Reg.* 6, (1853): 30; *Cal. of Va. State Papers*, 1: 235, 236.

Thomas Jefferson

George M. Curtis III

During the eleven years before Thomas Jefferson emerged as a leader of Virginia's Revolution, he devoted himself to a career in the law. Many of the hallmarks that people later associated with Jefferson's character—his prodigious capacity for work, his political and constitutional values, and his tenaciousness as an adversary—were products of those formative years when he established a professional standing in the colony and committed to paper notes of cases in the General Court which his executor published in 1829 as *Reports of Cases Determined in the General Court of Virginia.* Jefferson's preparation for the practice of law did not vary greatly from that of his contemporaries in Virginia. The difference appeared in his application to the task; here the scope of his learning and his dedication to self-improvement were unique. According to his college friend, John Page, Jefferson's voracious appetite for academic work surfaced early during his residence at the College of William and Mary, where he "could tear himself away from his dearest friends, to fly to his studies." The intensity of his scholarly habits was complemented by the close relationships that he established with several college teachers and later with his legal mentor, George Wythe.

Like many others, Jefferson most likely viewed legal education as a necessary foundation for a public life, which would encompass duties and opportunities that extended far beyond the practical confines of the profession. In 1762, when he began to study law with George Wythe, Jefferson was fatherless and without the prospect of an extensive inheritance. Law provided a natural avenue for enhancing his income as well as finishing his formal education. Furthermore, in Virginia the study and profession of law were considered a useful step to public service at both the county and provincial levels. Thus the law had practical, intellectual, and political applications.

Normally students of law in colonial Virginia apprenticed themselves to a lawyer, either in the country as did Edmund Pendleton's students in Caroline County or in town with such lawyers as George Wythe or Benjamin Waller. Training varied according to the dictates of the teacher and the inclinations of the students. Wythe did not subject Jefferson to the widespread practice of clerking in his office, for which Jefferson was grateful, calling such training "rather a prejudice than a help." Instead, Wythe introduced his student to the literature of the law, directing him what to read and in what general order. Furthermore, since Wythe did not insist that Jefferson do daily office chores, the student spent much of his time at his mother's home, Shadwell, where his own internal discipline dictated the study schedule. According to Dumas Malone, "he followed an appallingly rigorous program most of the time." Jefferson was proud of his habits, commenting later that "it is wonderful how much may be done if we are always doing." When asked for advice soon after completing the formal part of his education, Jefferson carefully spelled out a daily regime of reading and writing, in which reading law consumed the morning and the remainder of the day was given to perusing such less demanding subjects as politics, history, and literature. His blueprint for successful legal training continued what by that point had become a time-tested pattern for one who had determined "never to be idle." Little wonder that Jefferson later resented the meteoric rise of Patrick Henry, who had spent all of six weeks preparing for the bar.

Thanks to the commonplace books that Jefferson kept as an adjunct to his legal studies, there remains a clear picture of not only what he studied but also the order in which he read law. Wythe instructed Jefferson to begin with Sir Edward Coke's *Institutes of the Laws of England*, a work which the author admitted was "painful" but one which most teachers in Virginia believed to be the indispensable starting point. Jefferson quickly confessed that he indeed suffered. However, years later he acknowledged that the strenuous effort was worthwhile, adding that there had been political dividends attached to acquiring familiarity with the "black letter text," for in Jefferson's estimation "a sounder Whig never wrote." Following the first part of the *Institutes*, Coke's commentaries on *Littleton on Tenures*, Jefferson turned to reports of English cases. In succession, he read cases from the King's Bench reported by Andrews, Salkeld, and Lord Raymond as well as the remainder of Coke. Wythe had, in effect, designed a course for Jefferson in what law professors later would term the case method. Jefferson, having read the cases, briefed them in his commonplace book; this process, he later advised a prospective student, was a difficult but instructive exercise: "In reading the Reporters, enter in a commonplace book every case of value, condensed into the narrowest compass possible, which will admit of presenting distinctly the principles of the case. This operation is doubly useful, insomuch as it obliges the student to seek out the pith of the case, and habituates him to a condensation of thought, and to an acquisition of the most valuable of all talents, that of never using two words where one will do. It fixes the case, too, more indelibly in the mind."

Once he had begun to master the rudiments of English case law, Jefferson turned to a variety of law treatises and histories. Prominent among them were Lord Kames, *Historical Law Tracts* (1758); Sir John Dalrymple, *Essay Towards a General History of Feudal Property in Great Britain*; and Matthew Hale, *History of the Common Law*. When Blackstone's *Commentaries* became available sometime after 1770, Jefferson read the volumes with a growing sense of disappointment. Blackstone endorsed parliamentary supremacy at a time when Jefferson and other American Whigs were fast approaching a total denial of such a constitutional interpretation. Furthermore, Jefferson had derived from his reading of history and Coke a Whig interpretation of the development of English law. Therefore he suspected Blackstone's endorsement of what seemed to be extreme judicial discretion, limiting the power of juries and enhancing judges' power to interpret statutes.

Wythe's direction of Jefferson's legal education did not terminate with the reading program. Professionally and politically, he contributed to Jefferson's development by encouraging him to spend considerable time in Williamsburg. While there, Wythe's own intellectual influence was complemented by his introducing Jefferson to many contemporary political leaders including Governor Francis Fauquier and Edmund Pendleton, who had already earned the reputation of being the foremost advocate in the colony. It probably took little or no prodding from Wythe to persuade Jefferson to spend as much time as possible attending both the sessions of the House of Burgesses and the deliberations before the bar of the General Court. By the time he was admitted to the local and General Court bars in 1767, Jefferson had acquired the considerable benefits derived from the tutoring of one of the colony's most respected attorneys and the insights and prospects gathered from frequent exposure to Virginia's leading public figures.

Jefferson spent the better part of five years preparing for the legal profession, which he then practiced actively for only seven years. Beginning in 1774 his political activities commenced to command his full attention, and his public career would continue unabated until his retirement thirty-five years later from the new nation's highest elective office. The majority of those men beginning the practice of law in Virginia, through necessity or design, spent their early years establishing themselves in their home and neighboring counties. Jefferson was an exception to this rule insofar as he qualified for the bar of the General Court in the same year that he began his practice in the counties of Albemarle and Augusta. His county court practice flourished, and within a few years his General Court business indicated growing promise. Nowhere were Jefferson's technical skills and prospects for future clients indicated more clearly than in the correspondence he had with Thomas Burke, the Norfolk lawyer representing the estate of Henry Tucker. Between the middle of 1770 and the end of 1771, the two lawyers exchanged ideas for handling the complex issues of procedure connected with the litigation of Tucker's estate in the General Court. Jefferson's dedication to meticulous preparation and his determination to observe statutory regulations as they applied to docket process and rules of evidence revealed the high quality of his legal training and his aggressiveness as a young lawyer.

During the years that Jefferson attended the sessions of the General Court, it consisted of the governor and Council, men, as Jefferson noted, "chosen from along the gentlemen of the country, for their wealth and standing." Members of the court were usually not trained in the law which, according to David J. Mays, meant that they "lacked that nice discrimination with which trained judges approach complex problems." During the generation before the Revolution, however, several justices did have excellent legal training. William Byrd II, Lewis Burwell, Thomas Nelson, William Byrd III, and Robert Carter had all received legal training in England and had been admitted to the Inner Temple. During the years 1769-72 when Jefferson compiled his reports, Nelson, Carter, and William Byrd III were on the bench. In those cases where Jefferson mentioned the justices present and how they voted, the governor appeared only once, and in that instance he gave no opinion.

Complementing these justices was an array of astute lawyers practicing before the bar of the General Court. The rivalry of Edmund Pendleton and George Wythe was already famous within the legal fraternity. Other leading practitioners were John Randolph, the attorney general during the period of Jefferson's *Reports*, Peyton Randolph, Thomson Mason, Robert Nicholas, John Blair, Patrick

Henry, and Richard Bland. The justices whom these lawyers addressed constituted the criminal court of last resort
in Virginia, having original jurisdiction in capital crimes.
The General Court also had civil jurisdiction "to hear and
determine, all causes, matters, and things whatsoever relating
to or concerning any person or persons, ecclesiastical or civil,
or to any persons or things of what nature soever," whether
brought by original process or appeal, provided that original process issued for cases involving £10 or 2,000 pounds
of tobacco or more, according to the statute.

In the preface to his *Reports*, Jefferson revealed the under-
lying cause for his having reported the particular cases that
he did. Soon after he was admitted to practice in the General Court, Jefferson stated that he "began to commit to
writing some leading cases of the day, confining myself still
to those arising under our peculiar laws." The "peculiar
laws" of Virginia were those that dealt with definitions of
slavery and servitude, Indian rights, real property, and the
ecclesiastical jurisdiction of the General Court. In these
areas of law, Jefferson acknowledged what by 1768 had become a time-honored separation in the minds of Virginia
political and judicial leaders. The General Court's judgments "whether formed on correct principles of law [British
statutory law and common law precedent], or not, were of
conclusive authority. As precedents, they established au-
thoritatively the construction of our own [Virginia] enact-
ments, and gave them shape and meaning."

Jefferson advised his readers that his undertaking was in
part a continuation of similar efforts of such men as Sir John
Randolph, Edward Barradall, and William Hopkins to preserve some record of decisions of the General Court from 1730
to 1740. To illustrate the judgments of the generation preceding him to the General Court's bar, Jefferson devoted
the first half of his *Reports* to transcribing thirty cases selected
from those reported by Randolph and Barradall. The only
case to survive from Hopkins's now lost manuscript reports
is *Custis* v. *Fitzhugh*, which Jefferson copied. It is likely that

Jefferson copied these reports while he was practicing in the court since the manuscripts belonged to the last colonial attorney general, John Randolph. In at least two of the cases that he reported, Jefferson had more than a scholarly interest, for in both instances he was professionally involved in the litigation, either at the initial stages or in assisting George Wythe in preparing and presenting arguments in the General Court. These were *Howell* v. *Netherland* and *Godwin* v. *Lunan*. During a time before the commencement of official court *Reports*, Jefferson was, in effect, keeping notes on only those cases in which he himself had a professional interest. They became a useful extension of the cases and commentaries which he had already briefed in his commonplace book. During the brief period of his *Reports*, only eleven cases received Jefferson's attention; although his coverage was not as extensive as that of his predecessors, his *Reports* was much more complete in the rendering of the issues and the decisions.

An anonymous writer, reviewing the *Reports* soon after the volume's publication in 1829, lamented that "these cases were not published at an earlier period." If such had happened, subsequent courts could have relied upon certain judicial "landmarks" concerning rules of property. Since most of the cases Jefferson reported dealt with various Virginia slave laws, the reviewer stressed that the continuity of subsequent judicial decisions and legislative statutes would have been enhanced had these earlier cases been readily available. Considering that the reviewer was two constitutions, countless statutes, and over sixty years removed from these General Court decisions, his appeal indicated a fundamental reliance on the merits of the precedents that many of his contemporaries may well have repudiated. The laws regulating land transfer and descent had undergone such fundamental change in the years after 1776 that Jefferson himself may well have questioned the practical worth of publishing these colonial decisions. Furthermore, his political and constitutional perspective dictated against any overzealous devotion to precedents. It was not, after all, Jefferson who published these *Reports*, but Thomas J. Randolph, who had inherited the manuscript.

If the "black letter" value of Jefferson's *Reports* has faded in time, the historical worth has not. Until the publication of the reports of Randolph and Barradall in 1909, historians of Virginia's colonial General Court had no printed source available other than Jefferson's. More importantly, lurking in the arcane legal language are insights into the development of the legal profession and the maturing Virginia judiciary. Normally, professional accomplishments of the bar are revealed in several ways—knowledge and use of procedure, understanding of judicial and statutory precedents, and precision of legal reasoning. In several of the cases that Jefferson reported, *Blackwell* v. *Wilkinson, Robin* v. *Hardaway*, and *Carter* v. *Webb*, these qualities were clearly present on the part of the contending lawyers. Insofar as Jefferson indicated that his selection of cases was predicated in part upon their relevance to the development of Virginia law, the *Reports* contain examples of the explicit recognition by both the members of the bench and the bar of the discrepancies between English and Virginia law. This distinction was most clearly enunciated in cases involving slavery, where John Randolph in *Blackwell* v. *Wilkinson* could assert "there is no estate in England resembling that of slaves."

Perhaps the most notorious case exemplifying Virginia's maturing sense of an indigenous legal system was *Godwin* v. *Lunan*, which turned on the question of the extent of the ecclesiastical jurisdiction of the General Court. Jefferson assisted Wythe in this action against an incumbent pastor. Wythe, citing the 1748 statute which enumerated the jurisdiction of the General Court, argued that the general words in the statute's preamble established the court's "power of depriving ecclesiastics." Jefferson, however, sought to extend the argument further in order to distinguish ecclesiastical jurisdiction and the court's power to police the church. To cement his contention that the church existed at the pleasure of the state, Jefferson appended an essay discussing "Whether Christianity Is a Part of the Common Law?" to his *Reports*. The thrust of his argument focused upon the contention that members of Virginia's General Court, exercising the powers of the king's chancellor in the colony, were invested with the corollary power to sit as a "court of visitation" which could examine and remove from office any clergyman. Coming as it did on the heels of the public debate over control of minister's salaries, the fundamental issue in the Two Penny Act controversy, *Godwin* v. *Lunan* foreshadowed further deterioration of the independence of the Anglican church, which culminated in its disestablishment in the years after the Revolution.

Before the appearance in 1774 of Jefferson's influential pamphlet *A Summary View of the Rights of British America*, his education in the law, history, and politics had been extensive. The exercise of keeping notes on arguments in the General Court prepared him not only to assume political leadership during the Revolution but also to play a critical role in the revision of Virginia's laws after Independence. His later views on religious disestablishment, western land policy, the laws of descent, and slavery can in part be traced to his early work at the General Court both as a lawyer and as a reporter. The fruitfulness of Jefferson's ideas on public policies and constitutional principles stemmed from an intensive schooling and apprenticeship in the law. His *Reports*, which he neglected during later years, remain a double legacy—to the historian wishing to understand the operations of Virginia's colonial bar and bench and to students of the Enlightenment seeking to uncover the intellectual roots of one of America's most accomplished practitioners.

Sources: D. Malone, *Jefferson the Virginian* (Boston, 1948); M. D. Peterson, *Thomas Jefferson and the New Nation* (New York, 1970); J. P. Boyd, *Papers of Thomas Jefferson* (Princeton, N.J., 1950), vol. 1; G. Chinard, *Commonplace Book of Thomas Jefferson* (Baltimore, 1926); J. Waterman "Thomas Jefferson and Blackstone's *Commentaries*" in *Essays in the History of Early American Law* (Chapel Hill, N.C., 1969), ed. D. H. Flaherty; D. J. Mays,

Edmund Pendleton (Cambridge, Mass., 1952); L. Morton, *Robert Carter of Nomini Hall* (Williamsburg, 1941); "Jefferson's Law Reports" *Va. Literary Museum and Journal of Belles Lettres*, 1, no. 9 (1829): 129.

Charles Lee

W. Hamilton Bryson

Charles Lee, the son of Henry Lee and Lucy Grymes and brother of "Light-Horse Harry" Lee, was born in 1758 at Leesylvania, Prince William County. He entered the College of New Jersey (now called Princeton) in 1770 and received his A.B. in 1775 and an M.A. in 1778. In the next year he was reading law in Philadelphia, and in 1781 he was licensed to practice in Virginia.

From 1781 to 1795 Charles Lee practiced law in Alexandria. He was quite successful, having cases in all the courts of northern Virginia. It was during this period that he compiled his reports of Virginia cases. He was also politically active, holding the Virginia appointment of naval officer of the South Potomac from 1784 until 1789 when the position was suppressed upon the adoption of the Federal Constitution. He was the customs collector for the port of Alexandria from August 1789 to 1793, and from then until 1795 he represented Fairfax County in the Virginia House of Delegates. He was also admitted to the bar of Philadelphia in June 1794.

Lee's reports include cases in a variety of Virginia courts from 1784 to 1794. They were published in the *University of Richmond Law Review*, vol. 11, in 1977.

Charles Lee was an old personal friend of George Washington and shared his ardent Federalist views. Lee was appointed United States attorney general in November 1795 and was continued in office by John Adams. He remained attorney general until the Federalists lost political power in 1801. He was a close friend of Marshall, and they had the same political and judicial outlook. He was appointed to be one of the new circuit judges in March 1801, but the next year Congress repealed the Judiciary Act, and he along with the other Federalist "midnight judges" was removed from the bench. Lee then retired from the active political scene and devoted the rest of his life to his private law practice. He was counsel in *Marbury* v. *Madison* and aided in the defenses of Aaron Burr and Samuel Chase.

Lee was married twice, first in 1789 to Anne Lucinda Lee, the daughter of Richard Henry Lee; they had six children. His second wife was Margaret Christian Scott Peyton, who bore him three children. He spent his last days at his home in Fauquier County near Warrenton, and here he died on June 24, 1815.

Sources: *DAB*, s.v. "Lee, Charles"; *South in the Building of the Nation*, 12: 70-71; *Bull Fauquier Hist. Soc.*, 1st ser. (1923), pp. 243–45; Va. Hist. Soc. MSS 1, L 5113, a6, MSS 2, M 3817, a1; Swem and Williams, *Register of the General Assembly*, pp. 39, 41, 44; R. Sobel, *Biog. Directory of U.S. Exec. Branch* (Westport, Conn., 1971), p. 209.

John Brown

W. Hamilton Bryson

John Brown, the son of John and Judith Brown, was born on October 4, 1750, in or near Williamsburg. In March 1772, when he married Nancy Geddy, he was employed in the office of the secretary of the colony. Three years later he was appointed clerk of the court of Mecklenburg County and was sworn into office before the justices of that court on July 10, 1775. While in Mecklenburg he served as an officer in the Virginia militia. According to Frederick Johnston, "from the records left in his office, he was a good clerk, and everything [was] kept in good order."

In 1781 Brown was appointed clerk of the General Court of Virginia, which required him to move to Richmond. Therefore he appointed William Baskervill on June 4, 1781, to act as his deputy. He held the clerkship of Mecklenburg County until February 9, 1795, when he resigned to be succeeded by Baskervill.

N. G. Hutcheson, the present clerk of Mecklenburg County, writes: "some years ago I ran across a note made by my father, the late H. F. Hutcheson: 'John Brown (of Mecklenburg County) upon being appointed Clerk of the Supreme Court of Virginia, moved to Richmond. His residence faced on Broad Street and ran back on 9th Street to the little Catholic Church facing Grace Street. Mr. Brown was a good gardener and took a great deal of interest in the vegetables he grew in the back of his residence.'" In December 1792 Brown was elected a common councilman for the city of Richmond, but he declined to serve.

He held the clerkship of the General Court until 1794. In addition he was clerk of the Court of Appeals, the highest court of Virginia, from 1785 until his death in 1810. Apparently the Virginia appellate courts were not very busy before about 1795 for Brown was also the clerk of the District Court of Richmond during the period 1789 to 1797 and clerk of the court of chancery in 1787. It is probable that he was well supplied with deputies and clerks. It is easy to see why he was interested in the law of court costs, which was the main focus of his reports.

In 1795 he was appointed by the General Assembly to a committee which also included George Wythe, John Marshall, Bushrod Washington, and John Wickham. The duties of this group of eminent lawyers was to collect and superintend the printing of the Virginia acts concerning land. They requested the aid of Thomas Jefferson, who had the best collection of law books in the state, having purchased the libraries of Peyton Randolph and Richard Bland to add to his own books. Jefferson put his library at their disposal but suggested expanding the scope of the work to include all of the statutes of Virginia. This advice was accepted, and the General Assembly arranged several years later to have William Waller Hening edit the *Statutes at Large of Virginia*. In 1797 and 1798 John Brown was again associated with Marshall; this time he accompanied him to France on the XYZ Affair.

John Brown's reports cover cases in the Court of Appeals for the period 1791 to 1799. They were published in the *University of Richmond Law Review*, vol. 11, in 1977. They are primarily concerned with the problems of assessing court costs, other clerical matters, and the technicalities of appeals.

Brown acted as clerk of the Court of Appeals until his death in Richmond on October 31, 1810. He was buried the next day in St. John's churchyard. He was characterized in the *Virginia Patriot* shortly after his death as "long well known for his superior talents in the line of his profession, and highly esteemed for his urbanity of manners and general good deportment." He was survived by three sons and two daughters; one son, James Brown, was auditor of the Commonwealth for over forty years.

Sources: Univ. of Richmond Law Rev., vol. 11 (1977); F. Johnston, *Memorials of Old Va. Clerks* (Lynchburg, 1888), pp. 245, 329; *Cal. Va. St. Papers*, vols. 3-9, passim; A. Brown, *Cabells and Their Kin* (Richmond, 1939), p. 379; Hening's *Statutes*, 1: vii-xi. I would like to thank Charles T. Cullen, N. G. Hutcheson, Emily Jones, William Ray, and Lee Shepard for their assistance with the identification of John Brown and of his reports.

George Wythe

E. Lee Shepard

George Wythe was born on his father's plantation, Chester-ville, in Elizabeth City County in 1726. The early deaths of his parents deprived Wythe of any sustained formal education, but his mother worked hard to ground him in Greek and Latin before she died. After spending a short period of time at the College of William and Mary, most probably in the grammar school, Wythe went to Prince George County to read law with a relative, Stephen Dewey. Dewey neglected his young pupil, but Wythe managed to obtain sufficient knowledge to qualify as an attorney in the county court. Shortly thereafter, he moved to Spotsylvania County and began to practice law with John Lewis. Wythe strengthened his ties to the prominent Lewis family in December 1747 when he married Ann, daughter of Zachary Lewis. Unfortunately, his young wife died within a year of their marriage. Wythe remained in Spotsylvania for some eight years, building his legal practice and supplementing his still meagre knowledge of the law.

In the mid-1750s Wythe moved to Williamsburg and established a permanent residence. There he married Elizabeth Taliaferro, daughter of Richard Taliaferro of Powhatan, James City County. The death of his brother Thomas in 1755 assured Wythe of a sizable estate, which freed him to study law in earnest. He began to broaden his knowledge and his interests by reading widely in the classics and the liberal sciences, but he devoted most of his time to intensive study of both the civil and the common law. His legal practice mushroomed. He also began to devote himself to politics, serving temporarily as attorney general of the colony in the absence of Peyton Randolph in 1754 and then standing for election to the House of Burgesses, first from Williamsburg and later from Elizabeth City County. In the meantime, Wythe was admitted to the bar of the General Court, served as the mayor of Williamsburg, and became a member of the Board of Visitors of the College of William and Mary. In 1769 he abandoned his role as a representative and assumed the responsibilities of chief clerk of the House of Burgesses, a position he held until the Revolution.

Wythe played a prominent role in the Revolutionary political activity in Virginia. In 1775 he joined the other Virginia delegates to the Continental Congress in Philadelphia as a replacement for George Washington, who had assumed the position of commander-in-chief of the American army. Wythe supported independence for America and proudly affixed his signature to the Declaration drafted by his former law student, Thomas Jefferson. Then, like so many of his fellow Virginians in Congress, Wythe elected to return home to help to add the finishing touches to the political revolution taking place there. In 1777 Wythe returned to the General Assembly and was promptly elected Speaker of the new House of Delegates. This post he held for only a little more than a year when he was elected by the Assembly to be one of three judges of the newly established High Court of Chancery.

During this period Wythe embarked on one of the most significant projects of his legal career, that of serving on a committee, along with Edmund Pendleton and Thomas Jefferson, charged to review the laws of Virginia and bring them into conformity with the constitution of the newly independent state. Wythe's portion of the statutes concerned the period from the Glorious Revolution in England down to American Independence. The work required long and difficult evaluation of the laws. Finally a number of consolidated laws were presented to the Assembly by this committee, but not until 1785, under the leadership of James Madison, were most of these revisions adopted.

During the Revolution, the Board of Visitors of the College of William and Mary, prodded by Governor Jefferson, established a "Professorship of Law and Police." This was the first chair of law in an American college and came only twenty years after a similar chair had been established at Oxford for William Blackstone. George Wythe, who had become the most erudite legal scholar in Virginia, was the unqualified choice of the board to occupy this professorship. For over a decade Wythe served in this capacity, breaking ground in a very important field and setting precedents in the teaching of law that remain a part of legal education to this day.

Wythe returned to national politics for a short time in 1788 when he attended the Virginia convention for the ratification of the Federal Constitution. He was a quiet but persistent proponent of the federal scheme and helped to draft some of the proposed amendments which fostered ratification in Virginia. In the same year, with the reorganization of the Virginia court system, Wythe became the sole member of the High Court of Chancery. Edmund Pendleton and John Blair were moved up to the Supreme Court of Appeals. Wythe no longer would sit on the highest court in the state, but rather would have his decisions subjected to the scrutiny of able but nonetheless scholastically inferior judges.

Wythe's service as a law reporter came about in an unusual manner and was actually a direct result of the judicial reorganization. This reorganization, by placing Wythe in a subordinate position to Edmund Pendleton, provided the impetus for the renewal of an old rivalry. Pendleton and Wythe had both practiced law at the same time, often in the same courts, and in fact had often opposed each other in the trial of numerous civil suits. Pendleton, with his eloquent presentations to judges and jurors, regularly thwarted Wythe, whose arguments, though generally sound, were so complex that most juries and most members of the bench, who at the time happened almost always to be laymen, failed to grasp them. The rivalry was shelved during the Revolution when matters of larger consequence loomed over Virginia. While serving on the same court, Wythe and Pendleton seemed inclined to compromise, though occasionally Pendleton was outvoted by his colleagues. But differences between the two men were evident even then. Pendleton's decisions reflected a conservative nature; Wythe consistently sought to forge ahead and break new ground. Even when he supported Pendleton, Wythe frequently went several steps beyond what the president of the court had been willing to rule. Such was the case in 1782 in *Commonwealth* v. *Caton*. In this appeal on a treason conviction, Pendleton cautiously absolved the House of Delegates of any intention to violate the constitution by single-handedly issuing a pardon. Wythe went further. In a concurring opinion he stated emphatically that "if the whole legislature . . . should attempt to overlap the bounds, prescribed to them by the people, I in administering the public justice of the country, will meet the united powers at my seat in this tribunal; and pointing to the Constitution, will say to them, 'here is the limit of your authority; and hither shall you go but no further' " (4 Call 8). By taking these few steps further, Wythe enunciated for the first time the doctrine of judicial review.

Wythe's penchant for following his legal reasoning to its logical conclusions caused friction between himself and Pendleton, friction which exacerbated the tensions already existing between the two. Judicial reorganization simply added more fuel to the fire. David J. Mays estimated that between 1788 and Pendleton's death in 1803 more than one hundred fifty cases were taken on appeal from the Chancery Court to the Supreme Court of Appeals, and a majority of Wythe's decrees in these cases were modified or reversed. Mays noted that for "a sensitive man like Wythe, who had put all of his skill and love [for the law] into his opinions, this was unendurable." Wythe knew that once the Supreme Court ruled on appeals from his court there was no higher tribunal to which he or the litigants could go. That is what probably humiliated the chancellor most. Pendleton, his longtime rival, the man who had defeated him so often at the bar, now spoke the final word in all cases. Although Wythe knew he could never reverse the higher court's decisions, he could not stand idly by either. In 1795 "he gave vent to his indignation" by publishing a volume of reports entitled *Decisions of Cases in Virginia by the High Court of Chancery, with Remarks upon Decrees, by the Court of Appeals, Reversing Some of Those Decisions.*

These reports indicate just how erudite, how deeply learned in the law Wythe really was. The chancellor wrote his decisions without apology, assuming that the lawyers and judges who read them, despite their lack of structured training or full formal education, would be able to fully comprehend their meaning. And unlike many of his contemporaries, Wythe was not afraid to go beyond citing precedents and previously reported cases in his opinions. Foreshadowing the kind of approach brought to the law by the "Brandeis Brief," Chancellor Wythe ranged far and wide for support for his decisions and for examples to illustrate his points. He was not the least bit shy, for instance, of turning to the writings of antiquity to prove a point.

The reports also show another side of the man. Usually mild and friendly as an individual, always scrupulously impartial in cases he argued or tried, Wythe allowed himself to attack Pendleton in a merciless fashion. His unrestrainedly caustic *Remarks* were totally out of character for the man; and while they exhibited the frustrations of a scholar who loved and devoted himself to the law, they also showed that Wythe was not above manipulation. He arranged his reports so that the last case presented showed Pendleton in the very worst light. So virulent was this volume that Pendleton himself contemplated a rebuttal, but was dissuaded from such a project by his friends. As a law reporter, Wythe's career was short-lived. Once he aired his frustrations, the chancellor assumed a fatalistic attitude. Certain that his decrees would continue to be reversed by the higher court on a regular basis, Wythe simply resolved to continue to base his decisions on all the information at his disposal, and to carry his legal reasoning as far as it might lead, whatever the consequences.

After the first edition of his *Reports* in 1795, Wythe published fourteen additional opinions in pamphlet form. These are included in the scholarly edition of Wythe's *Reports*, which was issued in 1852 by Benjamin Blake Minor. This second edition, which is the appropriate one to be cited today, includes a memoir of George Wythe by the editor and an appendix containing the notes of William Green on several of Wythe's opinions. Minor's edition was reprinted in 1903 by the Michie Company.

Wythe resigned his chair at the College of William and Mary in 1790 when he moved to Richmond. Thereafter, he took law students into his own home, much the way he had welcomed Jefferson many years before. Several young aspiring lawyers such as John Breckinridge, Littleton Waller Tazewell, Spencer Roane, William Munford, and Henry Clay received instruction from the venerable sage of the law. When his death came in 1806, some believe by poison administered by a greedy nephew, Wythe had spent a full life in law. As lawyer, teacher, judge, legislator, and law reporter, Wythe had always shown his love for the law and his dedication to it.

Sources: W. Clarkin, *Serene Patriot: A Life of George Wythe* (Albany, 1970); J. Blackburn, *George Wythe* (New York, 1975); D. J. Mays, *Edmund Pendleton* (Cambridge, Mass., 1952), 2: 290–97; *DAB*, s.v. "Wythe, George"; L. G. Tyler, "George Wythe, 1726–1806," in *Great American Lawyers* (Philadelphia, 1907), 1: 51–90; A. D. Jones, "The Character and Service of George Wythe," *Proceedings of the 43rd Annual Meeting of the Va. State Bar Assn.* (1932), pp. 325–39; O. L. Shewmake, *The Honorable George Wythe, Teacher, Lawyer, Jurist, Statesman* (Richmond, 1950); W. E. Hemphill, "George Wythe the Colonial Briton: A Biographical Study of the Pre-Revolution Era in Virginia," Ph.D. diss., U. Va., 1937.

St. George Tucker

Charles T. Cullen

St. George Tucker was a native of Bermuda, born in 1752 into one of the island's most prominent families. His parents, Henry and Anne Tucker, sent three of their four sons to America: Thomas Tudor Tucker and Nathaniel Tucker became medical doctors in Charleston, South Carolina. Thomas was appointed treasurer of the United States by Thomas Jefferson in 1801. The youngest son, St. George, became interested in law and began reading in the office of his uncle, John Slater, the attorney general of Bermuda. His uncle was ill, however, and did not treat young St. George with much kindness. The experience of being in Slater's office was so disagreeable that St. George never got over his dislike of this method of learning law.

A combination of events determined St. George's ultimate departure from the island. Henry Tucker had met a Mr. Stark, probably Bolling Stark of Virginia, and had mentioned his son's desire to study law at the Inns of Court. Stark told Tucker's father about the College of William and Mary. He was impressed with what Stark said about "the regulations and great care that would be taken of education of the students as [well as] the cheapness of it," wrote Elizabeth Tucker to her brother in August 1770, "[and] I believe he has determined should you like it, to send you there." St. George's situation at Slater's was worsening, and he now complained of being "thick of hearing," a malady that plagued him throughout his life. By the end of the year, Henry Tucker had decided to send his son to Virginia as soon as possible.

St. George Tucker hoped ultimately to attend one of the Inns of Court, but it was clear that his father would not be able to send him in the foreseeable future. It was early in January 1772 when Tucker finally arrived in the small town of Williamsburg. He soon met several important members of the bar, and he became acquainted with the Randolph, Nelson, and Blair families. In spite of his father's pleas that he quickly proceed to the study of law, St. George followed a general course of study directed by the Reverend Thomas Gwatkin, professor of the school of natural philosophy and mathematics. Tucker also took courses in the school of moral philosophy, which embraced the study of rhetoric, logic, and ethics. Ethics included the study of natural and civil law. Generally, a student studied in these fields for four years in order to qualify for a Bachelor of Arts degree. Tucker did not intend to seek a degree and even took the basic courses over the objections of his father. St. George's uncle in Norfolk, Archibald Campbell, and the Reverend Mr. Gwatkin convinced the young student that he needed this foundation at the college before specializing in the study of law.

In the summer of 1772 Tucker left the college and began studying law under the direction of George Wythe, the eminent Williamsburg lawyer who directed the legal education of many of the colony's young men. As did all of Wythe's students, Tucker enjoyed a close association with his teacher. He used Wythe's library and worked as clerk in his office looking up cases and preparing legal papers. Tucker was expected to spend his spare time reading books on the law, such as those by Coke, Blackstone, Pufendorf, Montesquieu, and Burlamaqui. Frequently Wythe's students prepared arguments to present before each other in moot courts. When the General Court met they attended and took notes on arguments heard there. Wythe also introduced his students to members of the bench and bar, located as they were in the capital of the colony where the more advanced law cases were argued. Tucker was apparently a good student and learned law quickly.

After he had studied with Wythe for a few months, Tucker decided that if he could find a position for himself in Virginia he would stay. If not, he would try practicing in Bermuda using only what knowledge he had acquired under Wythe's training. One of Tucker's classmates happened to be Thomas

Nelson, Jr., whose father, as secretary of the colony, had the authority to fill vacant clerkships. In August 1773 Tucker asked to be appointed a clerk but, since vacancies were rare, he booked passage for Bermuda and returned to the island. He was soon back in Virginia, however, to accept appointment to the clerkship of Dinwiddie County. He spent the winter months reading law, and before setting out for his new job, he was examined and admitted to practice in the county courts in April 1774. (Clerks were permitted to practice in any court other than the one for which they worked). In reaction to the closing of the port of Boston, Virginia's leaders began closing the county courts in May 1774, just at the time Tucker was assuming his new position. Uncertain what to do, Tucker went to South Carolina in hopes of entering his chosen profession. From there he went to Philadelphia and back to Virginia. In a final attempt to establish a practice in Virginia, Tucker gained admission to the bar of the General Court during its April 1775 meeting. Unfortunately, this was the last session of the General Court to sit for three years. Tucker's licenses to practice law and his office as clerk were now useless. Out of money, he returned to Bermuda, where he was admitted to the bar. His business never prospered, however. In the summer of 1776 he decided to enter business with his father and oldest brother. Shipping goods from the West Indies to Virginia and other states was becoming very profitable, if dangerous. Tucker returned to Virginia in January 1777 to manage that end of the business. He soon found himself moving in directions that might have parted him from his chosen profession for good.

In 1778 St. George Tucker married Frances Bland Randolph, widow of John Randolph. In addition to her three sons, including John Randolph of Roanoke, the new Mrs. Tucker owned three plantations. The family moved to one of them, Matoax, in Chesterfield County, and Tucker began a new life of managing farms. When Lord Cornwallis's advancement into North Carolina threatened Virginia in 1781, Tucker joined the army as a major in Colonel Beverley Randolph's regiment. He soon became a colonel himself and, in the fall campaign at Yorktown, was a member of Governor Thomas Nelson's staff. His account of the battle and surrender remains one of the best sources of information about that pivotal event. After the British surrender, Tucker returned to his family in Chesterfield County and contemplated his future.

For a brief period after the war Tucker served on the Council of State, the governor's advisory council that in effect constituted the executive branch of state government. He next held several positions that could have been preparatory to a political career in the traditional manner. At the same time he began practicing in the county courts in the Petersburg area trying to become reaquainted with the law. It was as if he were trying to decide whether to pursue politics or law. By 1786 he had made his choice and began attending the state courts in Richmond.

Many changes had occurred in the state's laws and judicial structure since the Revolution. The General Assembly had appointed a commission to revise the laws and had restructured the court system to fit statehood. The revisal was not yet complete, but the court system had undergone fundamental change by 1786. The General Court had been retained as the state court with widest jurisdiction. The High Court of Chancery was made separate and the Court of Admiralty also had its own bench. The judges of these three courts met twice yearly as the Court of Appeals, the highest court in the state. Each of these courts met in Richmond in 1786, except admiralty, which continued to sit in Williamsburg. At this time St. George Tucker considered himself unprepared for the practice of law without first reviewing the legal treatises and new statutes and observing new court procedure closely. At least until later court reorganization, the General Court in 1786 was the most challenging for attorneys, and when court convened in April, Tucker was admitted to its bar.

Tucker spent his first terms learning the procedure of the court, listening to the more experienced attorneys argue their cases, and paying particular attention to the opinions rendered by the judges. It was especially important that he note new interpretations of the laws, for no official reports of the court were kept. One could learn what had been decided in any given case by going to the clerk's order books, but the reasoning used by the court in arriving at its decisions was not recorded there. Consequently, Tucker and other young lawyers took notes in court on cases that interested them. Tucker was careful to take particular notice of cases which gave new meaning to an old law. If a case contained no interesting legal points, he took very few notes. He also took advantage of the presence of the High Court of Chancery to attend its meeting and to take occasional notes on cases being heard there.

From time to time Tucker missed an important argument and obtained notes from one of the other young attorneys attending court. William Nelson was the source of several case notes in Tucker's collection. Sometimes Tucker had difficulty in hearing, a problem that plagued him throughout his life and forced him to supplement his notes with material from others.

After attending court for two years as an observer and occasionally as a practitioner, Tucker was elected a judge of the newly reorganized General Court in January 1788. This court was given a bench of ten judges who would ride circuit in pairs to hold district courts throughout the state. The jurisdiction of the court was roughly the same as the old General Court. The district court judges met en banc as the General Court to hear cases adjourned for difficulty or other specialized considerations. As the courts developed, the General Court became much less significant than it once had been and the district courts became very important in the overall judicial structure. Appeals now generally ran from the county courts to the district court and from there to the Court of Appeals. This decentralized system completed the reform of the state's judicial system begun in 1776.

St. George Tucker assumed his judicial duties at the spring term of 1789. During the following year, he received two additional appointments that became very important to him and to the legal history of the Old Dominion. The fall 1789 session of the General Assembly decided to appoint another commission to finish the revisal of the laws begun in 1776. Tucker was one of those selected to do the job, and he spent considerable time during the next three years collecting copies of statutes enacted by past assemblies, meeting with the other commissioners, and preparing a report to submit to the legislature. All previous attempts to finish this task had met with failure from the time Thomas Jefferson, George Wythe, and Edmund Pendleton prepared the first report in 1779 through at least two other efforts in the 1780s. The report prepared in 1792 was accepted by the General Assembly and was published in 1794 as the Revisal of 1792, although it was more a compilation of laws than a revisal. Tucker had wanted to do more in the way of revising old laws, but the legislature instructed the commission to do no more than compile the laws. In the end, therefore, Tucker's work received the thanks of the state but had little effect on the legal system.

George Wythe announced in 1789 that he expected to resign his position as professor of law and police at the College of William and Mary at the end of the term because he intended to move to Richmond where the High Court of Chancery met. St. George Tucker was at that time rector of the college's Board of Visitors and had moved to Williamsburg after the death of his wife in 1788. At the spring 1790 meeting of the board he resigned as rector in order to be chosen Wythe's successor. He began teaching in September 1790 and announced that he would use William Blackstone's *Commentaries on the Laws of England* as a text. His course became much more structured than Wythe's had been partly because it suited Tucker's nature to do so and partly because his lack of experience in teaching led him to rely more on printed materials than on informal methods of pedagogy. He supplemented Blackstone with lectures on such topics as United States and Virginia constitutional law and changes in property law effected on this side of the ocean. After teaching for several years, he decided to publish Blackstone's *Commentaries* in an American edition with his lectures added as appendices. He inserted footnotes to Blackstone's text indicating changes in the law as they had occurred, particularly in Virginia. This plan met with enthusiasm among Philadelphia publishers and the work appeared in five volumes in 1803. Tucker's Blackstone became a standard reference work for many American lawyers unable to consult a law library, especially those on the frontier. It is impossible to measure its impact on developing American law, but it is clear that sales were strongest in Virginia, as could be expected; it was also widely used in Pennsylvania and South Carolina.

Soon after publication of his edition of Blackstone, Tucker was elected a judge of the Court of Appeals to succeed Edmund Pendleton, who had died. He was the logical choice, and his only opposition in the General Assembly came from those members who thought it was time to give the western area of the state a seat on the state's highest court. Tucker resigned his professorship at the College of William and Mary, not entirely because of his new position in the judiciary but partly because he had begun to have serious disagreements with the Board of Visitors over how the college should be run. In any event, Judge Tucker began his new duties in Richmond at the spring term in 1804, although he refused to move his home from Williamsburg.

Just before Judge Pendleton died, the court was about to decide the important case of the glebes, *Turpin* v. *Lockett*, 6 Call 113. Had Pendleton lived long enough to vote in the case, it was clear he would have favored overturning the glebe law enacted at the 1801 General Assembly, thus ensuring a majority for that opinion and allowing the Episcopal church to retain its lands. The case became an important consideration of the legislature in choosing a successor for the departed judge, and Tucker's supporters let it be known that he would most likely vote in favor of upholding the constitutionality of the glebe law. This certainly helped secure the position for Tucker, and in 1804 he voted with Judge Spencer Roane in what would be viewed later as a rare alliance with that gentleman. The vote resulted in a tie because Judge William Fleming abstained. The glebe law was thus upheld.

Judge Tucker had kept notes on cases throughout his tenure as a district court judge, traveling around the state twice yearly and sitting with various colleagues, some of whom later sat with him on the Court of Appeals. Spencer Roane was such a judge; Tucker sat with him in 1792 and 1793 before Roane succeeded Henry Tazewell on the Court of Appeals in 1794. When the Court of Appeals convened in 1804, Tucker brought along his familiar notebook and continued taking notes at each session until his resignation in 1811. Toward the end of his career on the state judiciary, the court began meeting in conference to discuss cases before the bench. Tucker favored this development and fought for its continuance against Roane's strong opposition. Tucker took notes on conferences, thus providing modern researchers with a unique opportunity to view the inner workings of Virginia's highest court during this period. Unfortunately, Tucker's disagreement with Roane over this issue was only symptomatic of a larger, more fundamental difference between the two men. Roane was highly political and maintained close alliances with the state legislature. Tucker considered judges apolitical and throughout his life insisted that they should avoid any suspicion of political involvement. In 1810 the General Assembly, perhaps with Roane's influential support, lengthened the term of the Court of Appeals to such an extent that its members would find it necessary to live in Richmond or be almost constantly away from home if they lived elsewhere. Tucker saw through the stated purpose of the bill but lost his will to continue fighting with Roane. He resigned from the court on April 2, 1811.

Once retired to his home in Williamsburg, Tucker indulged his love of writing and composed essays, poems, and plays. He even planned a second edition of Blackstone's *Commentaries* and began making notes for it. His son Henry St. George Tucker was now an established attorney in Winchester about to embark on a congressional career. His young son Nathaniel Beverley Tucker had had great difficulty settling down in a highly competitive area of the state and was about to go to Missouri to find his place in the law. St. George Tucker planned to enjoy retirement with his second wife, Lelia Skipwith Carter, whom he had married in 1796.

President James Madison interrupted Tucker's plans by nominating him to become United States District Court judge for Virginia in 1813. Henry St. George Tucker urged his father to accept, and he reluctantly did so. Unfortunately for posterity, Tucker did not resume his habit of taking notes on cases coming before him, perhaps because most of the cases involved only questions of admiralty law.

In 1825 Daniel Call began collecting copies of reported decisions and notes on arguments before the Court of Appeals for a planned second series of printed reports. He wrote St. George Tucker and borrowed his 1,500-page manuscript of notes on cases. Many of Call's reported decisions in his third, fourth, and fifth volumes are printed directly from Tucker's reports with only slight editing. Some of the cases appearing in Tucker's notes were omitted by Call, suggesting the reporter exercised a degree of selectivity in his printed reports. Most marginal notations of Tucker's personal opinions of a lawyer or judge are consistently omitted, as are his notes on judicial conferences. Considering the amount of material Call printed from Tucker's notes, however, it is clear that his six-volume set would have been much smaller and less significant had Tucker been unwilling to lend his copious notes from his twenty-five years before the state courts of Virginia. Tucker's manuscript reports are presently being prepared for publication.

By 1825 Judge Tucker was an old man, and he decided to retire from the bench for good. He then returned to his second edition of Blackstone, but it was never completed. He died in 1827 while spending the summer at the home of his wife's stepson, Joseph C. Cabell, in Nelson County, Virginia.

Sources: M. H. Coleman, *Saint George Tucker* (Richmond, 1938); C. T. Cullen, "St. George Tucker and the Law in Virginia, 1772-1804," Ph.D. diss., U. Va., 1971.

John Mercer Patton, Jr.

James R. Cottrell

John Mercer Patton, Jr., was born into an established family at Springfield Farm near Culpeper on May 9, 1826. His father was an eminent lawyer and politician, serving as acting governor of the Commonwealth and as one of the revisors of the Virginia Code of 1849. The elder Patton's grandfather was General Hugh Mercer. Patton's mother, Margaret French Williams, was the daughter of Isaac Hite Williams, a well-known lawyer. The result was a significant social advantage for the younger Patton. He would receive a thorough education, marry well, and enter the legal profession. He was born into a society which he would grow to love fervently, risk his life defending, and never quite accept as vanquished following its destruction by the War Between the States.

Patton graduated from the Virginia Military Institute in 1846. It is not known what he did between 1846 and 1852, but it is safe conjecture that very soon after college, he moved to Richmond and began the practice of law. By 1852 he was a captain of the Richmond Light Infantry Blues. Patton's association with the Blues, the oldest military company in Virginia at that time, was as much an emblem of social prestige as it was a tribute to his military ability. Patton must have been a member of the Richmond bar by 1855, for in that year he and Roscoe B. Heath began their work as reporters for the Special Court of Appeals. On November 11, 1858, Patton married Sally Lindsay Taylor, a descendant of Zachary Taylor.

When Virginia seceded from the Union, Patton and six of his brothers entered the Confederate Army. Three of them served as officers with the Army of Northern Virginia. John commanded the Twenty-first Virginia Regiment, George

Smith Patton commanded the Twenty-second Virginia, and Waller T. Patton led the Seventh Virginia. The details of John Patton's military service can only be briefly sketched from available records. His early service was with Stonewall Jackson during the Valley campaigns. In 1862 he was commissioned a colonel of cavalry with orders to proceed to Richmond for duty with the Military Court. Two years later, he was back in the field commanding a battalion of hospital men on the intermediate line of fortifications protecting Richmond. Finally, on April 10, 1865, he was paroled from prisoner status at Appomattox Court House. It appears, therefore, that Patton served throughout the war until General Lee's surrender of the Army of Northern Virginia.

After the war, Patton retired to the Lindsay estate, The Meadows. During this period he maintained a regular correspondence with Francis H. Smith, superintendent of the Virginia Military Institute. The letters reveal an intense bitterness over the defeat of the South. Patton's resentment was so severe, in fact, that he resigned his position on the V.M.I. Board of Visitors rather than serve under the auspices of the Reconstruction government. In a letter dated September 13, 1865, Patton informed Smith of his decision: "I have realized, that if I continued to hold this office it would be under the bogus concern at Richmond. The idea that it would be necessary for me to qualify for this new appointment, and to take the abominable oathes required under this so-called new constitution has only recently occurred to me." There was another reason for Patton to be angry about the conditions with which he was forced to cope after the war. Patton revealed it in a letter to Smith in 1867: "You ask in [your] letter how many of the bonds of the V.M.I. [circulated to raise funds for the rebuilding of the Institute after its destruction by the Union Army] I will take. . . . . I have an earnest desire to do whatever I can for the V.M.I., with which I have so many sound associations. I have not however now, and have not had since the war ended, a surplus cent. I gave all my available resources to the Confederate cause . . . and have since (for the first time in my life) been struggling under a load of debt to work this plantation on."

Sometime after 1867, the Patton family moved to Ashland. Available records indicate that John resumed his practice of law in the 1870s. In 1870 and 1872 he was involved in the settlement of his grandfather's estate. During the same period, Patton brought an action against creditors of his father's estate. Both of these actions, as well as one brought in 1871 in regard to the Lindsay estate, involved the determination of heirs or the payment of creditors.

During his later years Patton, an Episcopalian, became very interested in religion, and published two theological essays. Just as he was no doubt influenced by his father to follow the law, two of his own sons, James Lindsay Patton and Robert Williams Patton, were guided to become Episcopal clergymen.

Patton's most important publication was the two volumes of reports of cases in the Special Court of Appeals which he edited in collaboration with Roscoe B. Heath. This court was established to alleviate the miserable backlog of cases then pending before the Supreme Court of Appeals. At the time it was created, the average appeal to the older court took seven years. On their own motion Patton and Heath were appointed official reporters to the Special Court of Appeals; their reports cover the period January 1855 to January 1857.

Simultaneously, Patton and Heath published their *General Index to Grattan's Reports*, which covered volumes two through eleven of those reports of the Supreme Court of Appeals. This index was published in 1856 in Richmond by West and is frequently found bound with the first volume of Patton and Heath's *Reports*.

Patton published in Wytheville in 1871 an *Address Delivered Before the Society of Alumni of V.M.I. on July 4, 1871*. This was essentially an exhortation against the policies of the Reconstruction era. It was reprinted in Richmond in 1873. He also wrote "Reminiscences of Jackson's Infantry," which appeared in the *Southern Historical Society Papers* 8 (1880): 139-42.

His first theological tract was his *Argument in Respect to the Validity of Ministerial Orders, in the Council of the Diocese of Virginia, at Alexandria, May 18, 1876* (Richmond: Clemmitt & Jones, 1876), 34 pp. Patton's largest work was *The Death of Death; or, A Study of God's Holiness in Connection with the Existence of Evil, in so far as Intelligent and Responsible Beings Are Concerned* (Richmond: Randolph & English, 1878, 210 pp.; 2d ed., London: Trubner, 1881, 252 pp.).

John Mercer Patton died at his home in Ashland on October 9, 1898. During his life he had fulfilled the roles of lawyer, soldier, farmer, theologian, and author. While his life can not be said to have been marked by the greatest of achievements, it was a full one characterized by diversity and lived according to the superior standards of the southern gentleman.

Sources: MS letters in V.M.I. Alumni Office; R. A. Brock, *Va. and Virginians* (Richmond, 1888), 1: 195, 196; M. Blumenson, *Patton Papers* (Boston, 1972), 1: 22; *DAB.*, s.v. "Patton, John Mercer"; Patton MSS at Va. Hist. Soc.; obit. in *Religious Herald*, Nov. 30, 1898.

Roscoe Briggs Heath

R. Earl Nance

Roscoe Briggs Heath was born in Petersburg on December 19, 1827, the second son of Hartwell Peebles Heath, a successful merchant, and Elizabeth Cureton Rives Heath. Nothing is known of Heath's early education, but his family obviously could afford to give him the best instruction available. In 1844 at age seventeen he received his Master of Arts from the University of Virginia. For the next year and a half he lived and read law with John Young Mason, who was at that time United States attorney general. This brought Heath into contact with many prominent and distinguished politicians, diplomats, and scientists of the day. Heath entered Harvard Law School in 1846 and received his Bachelor of Laws in June 1848.

Upon his graduation from law school, Heath, accompanied by his older brother Hartwell, embarked on an eighteen-month excursion to Europe, probably as a remedy for Roscoe's poor health. He returned to Virginia in 1849 and immediately began the practice of law in association with Mason in Richmond. The partnership, called Mason and Heath, prospered until 1853 when Mason was appointed American ambassador to France. Heath accompanied Mason to Paris and acted as his personal representative.

On May 29, 1855, Heath married Mason's daughter, Elizabeth Harris Mason, and soon thereafter he returned to Virginia and to the practice of law. His successes continued, and he was elected to the House of Delegates in 1857 to represent the city of Richmond.

The growing turbulence in American politics cut short Heath's budding legal and political career, and in spite of his frail physical condition and substantial opposition from his family, Heath volunteered for service in the Confederate Army in July 1861. Serving in Courtney's Regiment, an artillery brigade consisting mostly of Henrico County residents, Heath was Captain Courtney's administrative officer. However, in September 1861, Heath was promoted to captain and named assistant adjutant general and chief of staff for General Joseph R. Anderson, who was responsible for the defense of eastern North Carolina and the Virginia coast. Heath's poor health continued to handicap him to the point that immediately after participating in the successful defense of Richmond in the Seven Days' Battles, he was forced in September 1862 to leave the service and return to his Richmond home. Knowing he would never serve again, he resigned.

For nearly a year Heath was an invalid, unable to pursue even his scholarly interests. In this condition, Heath died on August 21, 1863. He left a widow and four small children at his death. Heath's literary collaborations with John M. Patton, Jr., which produced two volumes of reports and an index to several volumes of Grattan's reports, have been discussed in the sketch of Patton.

Sources: Mary M. Heath, "Genealogical Notes," MS in Va. Hist. Soc.; Nicholson Papers, Folder 28, MSS at College of Wm. and Mary; Swem and Williams, *Reg. of the General Assembly*, p. 180.

Robert Reid Howison

W. Hamilton Bryson

Robert Reid Howison, the son of Samuel and Helen Howison, was born in Fredericksburg on June 22, 1820. His father was a bank teller and notary public with a large family, but he was able to give Robert a superb secondary education in Fredericksburg on his limited means. Howison began grammar school at Hérard Academy, which was operated by a French veteran of the Napoleonic wars. At twelve he studied mathematics at the school of John Goolrick. This was followed by studies at the classical academy of Thomas H. Hanson where one of his fellow students was J. M. Patton, Jr.

At age fifteen Howison left school because his father felt unable to continue to favor him over his brothers, and he spent the next six years as a salesman, clerk, and bookkeeper in several Fredericksburg businesses. His evenings, however, were spent in reading, and in July 1838 he began Chitty's edition of Blackstone's *Commentaries*. This was the beginning of Howison's legal career; he describes it himself in his autobiography. "By the time I had completed the fourth book of Blackstone, the spirit of law had taken hold of me, and I no longer felt averse to the toils of study or the monotonies of practice. Blackstone, with all his transparent renderings of ancient lore, and his sensible reasons for artificial rules, had implanted in me the belief that 'the law is the perfection of reason.' "

He then spent the next three years reading law in his spare time. It is interesting to note the books which he studied; the following list gives them in the order in which they were read.

W. Blackstone, *Commentaries,* Chitty ed.

J. J. Burlamaqui, *Natural and Political Law*, Nugent trans.

J. Kent, *Commentaries*

H. St. G. Tucker, *Commentaries*

J. Story, *Equity Jurisprudence*

J. Story, *Conflict of Laws*

H. J. Stephen, *Pleading*

T. Starkie, *Law of Evidence*

W. Cruise, *Digest of the Laws Respecting Real Property*

J. T. Lomax *Digest of the Laws Respecting Real Property*

C. Fearne, *Contingent Remainders*

W. Roberts, *Fraudulent Conveyances*

C. Robinson, *Practice in the Courts of . . . Virginia*

H. Hallam, *History of the Middle Ages*

J. A. G. Davis, *Criminal Law . . . in Virginia*

In the fall of 1840 Howison entered the proprietary law school which Judge John Tayloe Lomax operated in Fredericksburg, and by the next spring he felt ready to apply for a license to practice. His application was successful, and in June 1841, at the age of twenty-one, he moved to Richmond and commenced the practice of law. However, just as he was becoming established at the bar, he felt a call to the ministry.

From 1842 to 1844 he studied at the Union Theological Seminary, which was then located seven miles south of Farmville in Prince Edward County. While there he was elected an honorary member of the Philanthropic Literary Society, a debating club at Hampden-Sydney College, and he also made the acquaintance of his future wife, the daughter of Dr. Samuel L. Graham, who was one of his professors.

In 1844 he accepted a call to the Staunton Presbyterian Church, but he had a nervous breakdown that winter, and he was forced to resign from the ministry. He returned to Fredericksburg to recuperate, and then later in 1845 he went back to Richmond to resume the practice of law. Here he prospered, and on November 24, 1847, he married Mary

Elizabeth Graham. In addition to his business at the bar, Howison made the time to write his two-volume *History of Virginia* (1846,1848), which earned for him in 1848 a corresponding membership in the Virginia Historical Society. In 1851 he published his *Reports of Criminal Trials*. His practice, which was in partnership with James N. Dunlop, was varied and successful, and in 1856 he was able to build a new house on Governor Street with a room in the basement for his law office. Many years later Judge George L. Christian described him as not "regarded as a very safe lawyer" but "certainly a fertile and ingenious one" with "a large and lucrative practice."

Howison was forty-one in 1861, and believing that he would not be of much use in the regular army, he found a Swiss soldier and paid him $1,000 to serve for him. Howison himself became a member of the Home Guard under Captain Potts and fought at Fort Gilmer, Seven Pines, and Fredericksburg. Later he served in the Office of the Adjutant General in Richmond.

After the war his law practice revived, and he was doing as well as could be expected for the times, 1865 to 1870. In 1870 he had the misfortune to be in the middle of the Capitol Disaster, when the overcrowded courtroom collapsed just before the decision in the *Richmond Mayoralty Case*. Howison was rescued from the rubble and sustained only minor physical injuries. However, the accident brought on a severe mental depression which caused him to give up his practice. He moved to his farm Braehead near Fredericksburg to recuperate.

He resumed the practice of law in 1875 in Fredericksburg where he could continue to live on his farm, which was apparently required for his nerves. In 1880 he decided to give up the law and return to the Presbyterian ministry, and for the next three years he commuted on the weekends to three small churches in Hanover County. In May 1883 he went to the Third Presbyterian Church on Church Hill in Richmond. This, of course, necessitated a move back to Richmond. Six years of city life was apparently all that he could stand, and so he resigned so that he could return to Brae-head. He went back to commuting to various churches, first to Sharp's Wharf in Richmond County, then to Culpeper and Orange, then Ashland.

During this period his activities in historical scholarship continued unabated. In 1892 he published his *History of the United States*, and in 1894 he accepted a lectureship in American history at the College of Fredericksburg. That same year saw his election as an honorary member of the Columbia Historical Society of Washington, D.C.; three years later he was awarded a doctorate of laws by Hampden-Sydney College.

Howison's *Reports of Criminal Trials* was the only one of his many publications to be of a legal nature. This thin volume appeared in 1851 and reports eight trials in the circuit court of Henrico County and two from the federal court for the Eastern District of Virginia. These reports are unique in that they are the only printed ones of criminal trials in Virginia. They, of course, have little value as precedent and were thus largely forgotten, but from a historical point of view, they give us a rare peek at the criminal procedures of the 1850s.

Howison's first historical work was his *History of Virginia*. The first volume, which was published in Philadelphia in 1846, begins with the European explorations to North America and ends with the year 1763. Volume two appeared in 1848, published in Richmond, and continues the narrative up to 1847. The work concludes with a description of the Commonwealth in 1847. In his autobiography, Howison mentions that he made $450 from it. At this same time he contributed biographical sketches of Generals Gates, Morgan, and Marion to a work edited in 1847 by R. W. Griswold, *Washington and the Generals in the American Revolution*.

His next work was the *History of the War* (between the States), which appeared in installments in the *Southern Literary Messenger* between February 1862 and June 1864. It began with a thorough discussion of the background of the war, sectional jealousies, and slavery. Howison got only as far as the first months of 1862 in his narrative before the shortage of paper killed this celebrated journal. "Fredericksburg in the War" appeared in the transactions of the Southern Historical Society for 1875, pp. 9-17, which were printed in the *Southern Magazine*, vol. 16.

In 1880 Howison presented a paper to the Fredericksburg Library and Lyceum Association on the history of their city. This was published under the title *Fredericksburg: Past, Present and Future*. A second edition with a supplement bringing it up to date was issued in 1898. In 1892 he completed his *History of the United States of America*, which was written for the use of students. It is a large work of 919 pages and includes the first month of 1892.

In 1883 Howison won a prize for his essay on the necessity of maintaining a high level of education for preachers, "The New Testament Plan of Educating Candidates for the Christian Ministry." This was published in October 1883 in the *Southern Presbyterian Review*, vol. 34, pp. 651-682. In this same year his major religious work, *God and Creation*, appeared. To his great chagrin it was censured by the local presbytery on a minor theological point. However, he suffered no loss of personal prestige or respect. In 1887 Howison along with George D. Armstrong and Hugh Blair published a *Historical Sketch of the Presbytery of East Hanover, Virginia*, which they had been appointed by the presbytery in the preceding year to write.

In 1901 he finished writing his autobiography, "Twice Forty Years of American Life." This is an interesting though rambling work. As one would expect it is full of namedropping, but there are many interesting comments on the celebrated events and personalities of his times, politicians and lawyers, Dickens, Jenny Lind, Prescott, Lee. The table of contents of this manuscript was given in the *William and Mary Quarterly*, 1st ser. 26 (1918): 217, 218. Chapter two, "Fredericksburg, Her People and Characters," was printed in the same journal, 2d ser. 2 (1922): 221-38. A part of chapter six "Duelling in Virginia," appeared in the *Quarterly,* 2d ser. 4 (1924): 217-44. Omitted were the later duels, most notably that between Mordecai and McCarty in the 1870s.

In 1903 ill health forced him to resign his lectureship. He was the father of one son and two daughters. He died on November 1, 1906, in Fredericksburg, having made his mark as a lawyer, minister, and historian.

Sources: R. R. Howison, "Twice Forty Years of American Life" (his autobiography) MS at College of Wm. and Mary; *Va. L. Reg.* 14 (1909): 747; *Wm. & Mary Qtly.* 1st ser. 26 (1918): 217; *South in the Building of the Nation,* 11: 522, 523; *National Cyclopedia of Am. Biog.* 19 (1926): 302, 303.

Appendixes

Appendix I

Table of the Editions of the Virginia Reports

This table gives the standard renumbering of the Virginia reports, the original volume number and the standard abbreviation of the volume, the city of publication, the publisher, and the date of publication.

1 Va.	1 Wash.	Richmond	Nicolson	1798
		Philadelphia	Small	1823
		Charlottesville	Michie	1903
2 Va.	2 Wash.	Richmond	Nicolson	1799
		Philadelphia	Small	1823
		Charlottesville	Michie	1903
3 Va.	1 Va. Cas.	Philadelphia	Webster	1815
		Richmond	Randolph	1853
		Charlottesville	Michie	1902
4 Va.	2 Va. Cas.	Richmond	Cottom	1826
		Charlottesville	Michie	1902
5 Va.	1 Call	Richmond	Nicolson	1801
		Richmond	Cottom	1824
		Richmond	Morris	1854
		Charlottesville	Michie	1902
6 Va.	2 Call	Richmond	Nicolson	1802
		Richmond	Cottom	1824
		Richmond	Morris	1854
		Charlottesville	Michie	1902
7 Va.	3 Call	Richmond	Nicolson	1805
		Richmond	Cottom	1824
		Richmond	Morris	1854
		Charlottesville	Michie	1902
8 Va.	4 Call	Richmond	Smith	1833
		Charlottesville	Michie	1902
9 Va.	5 Call	Richmond	Smith	1833
		Charlottesville	Michie	1902
10 Va.	6 Call	Richmond	Smith	1833
		Charlottesville	Michie	1902
11 Va.	1 Hen. & M.	Philadelphia	n.p.	1808
		Flatbush, N.Y.	Riley	1809
		Charlottesville	Michie	1903

12 Va.	2 Hen. & M.	Flatbush, N.Y.	Riley	1809
		Charlottesville	Michie	1903
13 Va.	3 Hen. & M.	New York	Riley	1810
		Charlottesville	Michie	1903
14 Va.	4 Hen. & M.	New York	Riley	1811
		Charlottesville	Michie	1903
15 Va.	1 Munf.	New York	Riley	1812
		Charlottesville	Michie	1903
16 Va.	2 Munf.	New York	Riley	1814
		Charlottesville	Michie	1903
17 Va.	3 Munf.	New York	Riley	1816
		Charlottesville	Michie	1903
18 Va.	4 Munf.	Philadelphia	Webster	1817
		Charlottesville	Michie	1904
19 Va.	5 Munf.	Fredericksburg	Gray	1819
		Charlottesville	Michie	1904
20 Va.	6 Munf.	Richmond	Pollard	1821
		Charlottesville	Michie	1904
21 Va.	Gilm.	Richmond	Pollard	1821
		Charlottesville	Michie	1903
22 Va.	1 Rand.	Richmond	Cottom	1823
		Charlottesville	Michie	1904
23 Va.	2 Rand.	Richmond	Cottom	1824
		Charlottesville	Michie	1904
24 Va.	3 Rand.	Richmond	Cottom	1826
		Charlottesville	Michie	1904
25 Va.	4 Rand.	Richmond	Cottom	1827
		Charlottesville	Michie	1904
26 Va.	5 Rand.	Richmond	Cottom	1828
		Charlottesville	Michie	1904
27 Va.	6 Rand.	Richmond	Shepherd	1829
		New York	Gold	1832
		Richmond	Walker	1875
		Charlottesville	Michie	1904
28 Va.	1 Leigh	Richmond	Shepherd	1830
		Richmond	Ritchie & Dunnavant	1854
		Charlottesville	Michie	1903
29 Va.	2 Leigh	Richmond	Shepherd	1831
		Richmond	Ritchie & Dunnavant	1856
		Charlottesville	Michie	1903

30 Va.	3 Leigh	Richmond	Shepherd	1833
		Richmond	Ritchie &	
			Dunnavant	1857
		Charlottesville	Michie	1903
31 Va.	4 Leigh	Richmond	Shepherd	1834
		Richmond	Ritchie &	
			Dunnavant	1858
		Charlottesville	Michie	1903
32 Va.	5 Leigh	Richmond·	Shepherd	1836
		Richmond	Ritchie &	
			Dunnavant	1863
		Charlottesville	Michie	1903
33 Va.	6 Leigh	Richmond	Shepherd &	
			Colin	1837
		Richmond	Gary &	
			Clemmitt	1867
		Charlottesville	Michie	1903
34 Va.	7 Leigh	Richmond	Shepherd &	
			Colin	1838
		Richmond	Gary &	
			Clemmitt	1867
		Charlottesville	Michie	1903
35 Va.	8 Leigh	Richmond	Shepherd &	
			Colin	1839
		Richmond	Walker	1872
		Charlottesville	Michie	1903
36 Va.	9 Leigh	Richmond	Shepherd &	
			Colin	1840
		Richmond	Walker	1872
		Charlottesville	Michie	1902
37 Va.	10 Leigh	Richmond	Shepherd &	
			Colin	1841
		Richmond	Walker	1873
		Charlottesville	Michie	1902
38 Va.	11 Leigh	Richmond	Shepherd &	
			Colin	1842
		Richmond	Walker	1873
		Charlottesville	Michie	1902
39 Va.	12 Leigh	Richmond	Shepherd &	
			Colin	1844
		Richmond	Walker	1875
		Charlottesville	Michie	1902
40 Va.	1 Rob.	Richmond	Shepherd &	
			Colin	1843

		Richmond	Walker	1874
		Charlottesville	Michie	1902
41 Va.	2 Rob.	Richmond	Shepherd & Colin	1844
		Richmond	Walker	1875
		Charlottesville	Michie	1902
42 Va.	1 Gratt.	Richmond	Shepherd & Colin	1845
		Richmond	Ritchie & Dunnavant	1860
		Richmond	O'Bannon	1895
		Charlottesville	Michie	1902
43 Va.	2 Gratt.	Richmond	Shepherd & Colin	1846
		Richmond	Ritchie & Dunnavant	1861
		Richmond	O'Bannon	1894
		Charlottesville	Michie	1902
44 Va.	3 Gratt.	Richmond	Shepherd & Colin	1847
		Richmond	Schaffter	1871
		Richmond	O'Bannon	1897
		Charlottesville	Michie	1902
45 Va.	4 Gratt.	Richmond	Shepherd & Colin	1848
		Richmond	Schaffter	1871
		Richmond	O'Bannon	1897
		Charlottesville	Michie	1902
46 Va.	5 Gratt.	Richmond	Colin	1849
		Richmond	Schaffter	1871
		Richmond	O'Bannon	1898
		Charlottesville	Michie	1902
47 Va.	6 Gratt.	Richmond	Colin, Baptist, Nowlan	1850
		Richmond	Schaffter	1871
		Richmond	O'Bannon	1898
		Charlottesville	Michie	1902
48 Va.	7 Gratt.	Richmond	Colin & Nowlan	1852
		Richmond	O'Bannon	1894
		Charlottesville	Michie	1902
49 Va.	8 Gratt.	Richmond	Colin & Nowlan	1852

		Richmond	O'Bannon	1893
		Charlottesville	Michie	1902
50 Va.	9 Gratt.	Richmond	Ritchie &	
			Dunnavant	1854
		Richmond	O'Bannon	1893
		Charlottesville	Michie	1902
51 Va.	10 Gratt.	Richmond	Ritchie &	
			Dunnavant	1855
		Richmond	O'Bannon	1892
		Charlottesville	Michie	1902
52 Va.	11 Gratt.	Richmond	Ritchie &	
			Dunnavant	1855
		Richmond	O'Bannon	1892
		Charlottesville	Michie	1902
53 Va.	12 Gratt.	Richmond	Ritchie &	
			Dunnavant	1856
		Richmond	O'Bannon	1891
		Charlottesville	Michie	1902
54 Va.	13 Gratt.	Richmond	Ritchie &	
			Dunnavant	1857
		Richmond	O'Bannon	1891
		Charlottesville	Michie	1902
55 Va.	14 Gratt.	Richmond	Ritchie &	
			Dunnavant	1859
		Richmond	O'Bannon	1889
		Charlottesville	Michie	1902
56 Va.	15 Gratt.	Richmond	Ritchie &	
			Dunnavant	1860
		Richmond	O'Bannon	1889
		Charlottesville	Michie	1902
57 Va.	16 Gratt.	Richmond	Randolph	1867
		Richmond	O'Bannon	1895
		Charlottesville	Michie	1901
58 Va.	17 Gratt.	Richmond	Fore	1867
		Richmond	O'Bannon	1896
		Charlottesville	Michie	1901
59 Va.	18 Gratt.	Richmond	Fergusson &	
			Rady	1868
		Richmond	O'Bannon	1896
		Charlottesville	Michie	1901
60 Va.	19 Gratt.	Richmond	Schaffter	1870
		Richmond	O'Bannon	1900
		Charlottesville	Michie	1901

61 Va.	20 Gratt.	Richmond	Schaffter	1871
		Charlottesville	Michie	1901
62 Va.	21 Gratt.	Richmond	Walker	1872
		Charlottesville	Michie	1901
63 Va.	22 Gratt.	Richmond	Walker	1873
		Charlottesville	Michie	1901
64 Va.	23 Gratt.	Richmond	Walker	1874
		Charlottesville	Michie	1901
65 Va.	24 Gratt.	Richmond	Walker	1875
		Charlottesville	Michie	1901
66 Va.	25 Gratt.	Richmond	Walker	1875
		Charlottesville	Michie	1901
67 Va.	26 Gratt.	Richmond	Walker	1876
		Charlottesville	Michie	1901
68 Va.	27 Gratt.	Richmond	Walker	1877
		Charlottesville	Michie	1901
69 Va.	28 Gratt.	Richmond	Walker	1878
		Charlottesville	Michie	1900
70 Va.	29 Gratt.	Richmond	Frayser	1878
		Charlottesville	Michie	1900
71 Va.	30 Gratt.	Richmond	Frayser	1879
		Charlottesville	Michie	1900
72 Va.	31 Gratt.	Richmond	Walker	1880
		Charlottesville	Michie	1900
73 Va.	32 Gratt.	Richmond	Walker	1880
		Charlottesville	Michie	1900
74 Va.	33 Gratt.	Richmond	Walker	1881
		Charlottesville	Michie	1900
75 Va.		Richmond	Walker	1882
		Richmond	O'Bannon	1900
		Charlottesville	Michie	1908
76 Va.		Richmond	Walker	1883
		Richmond	O'Bannon	1900
		Charlottesville	Michie	1908
77 Va.		Richmond	Derr	1884
		Richmond	O'Bannon	1900
		Charlottesville	Michie	1921
78 Va.		Richmond	Derr	1884
		Charlottesville	Michie	1915
79 Va.		Richmond	Derr	1885
		Charlottesville	Michie	1915
80 Va.		Richmond	Micou	1886
81 Va.		Richmond	Micou	1887
		Charlottesville	Michie	1909

82 Va.	Richmond	O'Bannon	1888
	Charlottesville	Michie	1909
83 Va.–103 Va.	Richmond	O'Bannon	1888–1905
104 Va.-148 Va.	Richmond	Bottom	1906–1928
149 Va.–date	Richmond	Va. Division of Purchase and Printing	1928–date
1 VCD	Boston	Boston Book Co.	1909
2 VCD	Boston	Boston Book Co.	1909
Jeff.	Charlottesville	Carr	1829
	Charlottesville	Michie	1903
Wythe	Richmond	Nicolson	1795
	Richmond	Randolph	1852
	Charlottesville	Michie	1903
1 Pat. & H.	Richmond	West	1856
	Charlottesville	Michie	1902
2 Pat. & H.	Richmond	West	1857
	Charlottesville	Michie	1902
Howison	Richmond	West	1851
	New York	Warren	1937
1 Va. Dec.	Charlottesville	Michie	1902
2 Va. Dec.	Charlottesville	Michie	1902

Since 1887 Virginia cases have also been published in the *South Eastern Reporter*, St. Paul, Minn.: West, 1887 to date.

Reporters:

James Muscoe Matthews, 1882
George W. Hansbrough, 1883–1895
Martin Parks Burks, 1896–1917
Thomas Johnson Michie, 1917–1937
Addinell Hewson Michie, 1937–1953
Charles Killian Woltz, 1953–1967
Charles Marshall Davison, Jr., 1967–date

Miscellaneous reports from Virginia trial courts:

Decisions of Judge J. Singleton Diggs of Corporation Court of Lynchburg, Va., n.p., n.d.

Five cases from 1890 to 1893 on points not settled by the Supreme Court
of Appeals.

Opinions of Brockenbrough Lamb, 2 vols., Richmond: First and Merchants
National Bank, 1955, 1964.

Cases from 1942 to 1963 in the Chancery Court of the City of Richmond.

Hughes's Kentucky Reports include some Virginia cases from June 1785
to March 1792.

Appendix II

Advance Sheets in Virginia

The practicing attorney always wants to have at his fingertips the most recent statement of the law. To satisfy this need advance sheets are issued as soon as several opinions have been rendered, and thus the lawyer is not forced to wait until enough have been collected to fill an entire permanent volume of reports. The first attempt to supply the Virginia bar with advance sheets was made by William Waller Hening and William Munford in 1807. The first volume of their joint effort at reporting Virginia cases was issued to subscribers in three installments, one after each of the terms of the Supreme Court of Appeals. At the end of the year they supplied a new title page, preface, table of cases, and index, and the subscriber bound these and the advance sheets together to make the permanent volume. Unfortunately in the next year the terms of the court were rearranged, and from a printing standpoint this sytem was rendered no longer feasible. However, the idea was good and the lawyers' need remained. In fact in 1819 Munford was criticized for being slow in reporting the decisions of the court, and an official court reporter was appointed to see that the job was done properly and quickly.

It was not until the beginning of 1856 that the Virginia bar was again served by any advance reporting of cases. In that year the first law journal of Virginia, the *Quarterly Law Journal*, was published in Richmond by A. B. Guigon. The major purpose of this venture appears to have been the advance publication of selected Virginia cases. There were also articles and reports from other juris-dictions. This journal was succeeded in format and in purpose by the *Quarterly Law Review* in 1860. This journal, which was edited by A. H. Sands, ceased to appear after the April 1861 issue, being an early casualty of the invasion of Federal troops.

After Virginia had recovered from the war and Reconstruction, a new effort at periodical legal scholarship was launched. In 1877 the *Virginia Law Journal* appeared, and the policy of the two earlier journals of reporting selected cases was reestablished. This journal folded in 1893, but its successor in 1895, the *Virginia Law*

Register, continued to function as a selective advance reporter for Virginia cases. From 1895 to 1904 the cases were selected and reported for this journal by M. P. Burks, the official state reporter. The *Virginia Law Register* continued to print opinions of the Virginia Supreme Court of Appeals after 1904, but the quantity constantly declined until the demise of the journal in 1927, no doubt reflecting the competition from other publishers to supply advance sheets for Virginia.

The systematic publication of advance sheets for all of the opinions of the Supreme Court of Appeals began in 1887 when the West Publishing Company inaugurated their *South Eastern Reporter*. In 1899 the short-lived *Virginia Supreme Court Reporter* was begun; this provided advance sheets in only three volumes over a period of three years. In 1907 William Wallace Scott and Maury Baldwin Watts established the series of advance sheets called *Virginia Appeals*. Watts was the sole reporter for volumes two through thirty-five, the last of which appeared in 1926. The official Virginia advance sheets were issued as early as 1944,[1] and they have been published ever since.

---

[1] I would like to thank Alan T. Gravitt for supplying me with this date.